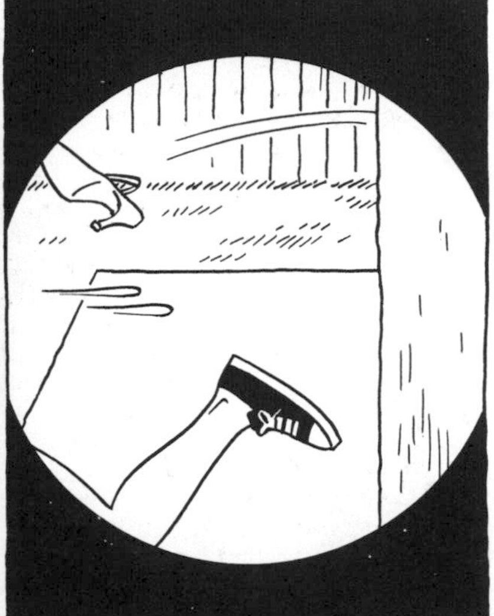

--FUCK--- SUMMER!

XAIME 13

1.

FUCK SUMMER AND ALL ITS LIES...

BONK
SONG'S OVER.

F-F-F-FUCK SU
THERE IT GOES AGAIN.

YOU SAID ERIC LOPEZ INVITED YOU TO HEAR OOOT PRACTICE, TONTA.
YOU CAN HEAR THEM PRACTICING, CANTCHA?

THEY'RE JUST PLAYING THE SAME OLD SONG OVER AN' OVER...
WE COULD HAVE BEEN AT THE MOVIE.
CAN WE STILL GO?
I'M NOT GOING TO NO LAME TWILIGHT MOVIE!

MOM GAVE US MONEY FOR THE TICKETS AN' RED VINES. WHEN DOES SHE EVER DO THAT?
WHEN SHE WANTS US AS FAR FROM THE HOUSE AS POSSIBLE.
HAVE FUN AT YOUR MOVIE, TWI-TARDS!
2.

SUMMER POSSIBILITI

SUMMER CAN JUST FUCK OFF!!!

CLOSED PRACTICE.
FOR YOU.
HEY, POLICE! OPEN UP!

HEY, WHAT TOOK YOU GUYS SO LONG?
I HOPE YOU MISSED US, NOT THE BEER.
I HAD TO BUY FILM!
HA HA!

HI, ERIC!
HEY, TONTA. WHAT ARE YOU DOING OUT HERE?

OH, YOU KNOW, JUST HANGIN'.
OOPS! HEH.
SHUT THE FUCKIN' DOOR ALREADY!

OK, LET'S FUCKIN' GO AGAIN...
CLICK! CLICK! CLICK! CLICK!

3.

YEAH, IT TOTALLY BITES. AT SCHOOL WE GOTTA WEAR THIS UNIFORM...

IT'S LIKE, THIS POLO SHIRT AND THIS SKIRT AND THE SKIRTS ARE LIKE, DOWN TO HERE LIKE, SOMEBODY'S GRANDMA MADE 'EM, SO EVERYBODY OF COURSE LIKE, HEMS 'EM...

SOME, LIKE MINE ARE UP TO HERE BUT SOME GIRLS HEM 'EM WAY UP TO HERE LIKE A CHEERLEADER AND YOU CAN SEE THEIR BUTTCHEEKS SOMETIMES, Y'KNOW...

BUT THEN MOST GIRLS WEAR SHORTS UNDERNEATH. I THINK THERE'S ONLY ONE GIRL IN MY WHOLE SCHOOL THAT DOESN'T HEM HER SKIRT, BUT SHE'S JUST WEIRD ANYWAY...

SOMEBODY SAID THAT SHE DOESN'T WEAR ANYTHING UNDER THERE BUT I'M LIKE, WHO GIVES A SHIT? TO EACH HIS OWN, Y'KNOW? IT'S COOL, WHATEVS...

I MEAN...
UH...

MOBAND

4.

SCREE
HONK!
CRUNCH!

MOSES!
HEY, TONTA. DID YOU BRING MY BOARD?

HOW DID YOUR SKATE DATE PICNIC OUTING PLAN GO WITH ERIC LOPEZ?
HE HAD TO PRACTICE. OOOT'S RECORDING AN E.P. SOON.

OH, YEAH. CHATA WAS BRAGGING 'CAUSE SHE GETS TO TAKE PHOTOS FOR IT.
YUP.

FUCK THOSE ROCKSTARS. ZERO PUSSY'S BETTER ANYWAY.
YEH...

SO, DID YOU BRING MY BOARD BACK?
EH...

WHY ARE WE GOING BACK FOR IT? IT'S PROBABLY BROKEN INTO A MILLION PIECES.
YEAH, BUT I CAN PROBABLY SALVAGE THE TRUCKS AN' WHEELS.

I TOLD YOU, I'LL JUST BUY YOU A BRAND NEW ONE.
YEAH? WHERE ARE YOU GONNA GET THE MONEY, FROM YOUR MOM WHO YOU SAY TOTALLY HATES YOU, OR FROM AL "HE'S NOT MY DAD" CASTOR?

AL WOULD TOTALLY GIVE IT TO ME IF I ASKED HIM.
JUST FOR THAT, I'M NOT GONNA TELL YOU WHERE YOUR BOARD GOT STEAMROLLED. YOU GOTTA FIND IT YOURSELF.
I SEE IT!

HEY, IT'S NOT TOO BAD. A LITTLE CRACKED BUT STILL RIDEABLE.
I GUESS YOU AN' AL ARE OFF THE HOOK, TONTA.
FFT...
AH, I'M JUST DOGGIN' YA.
6.

WHAT WERE YOU DOING IN THIS PART OF TOWN? ITS SO FAR OUT OF THE WAY FROM OOOT PRACTICE AN' MY HOUSE.
JUST RIDING WHERE THE SIDEWALK TOOK ME. MUST BE THE LONER IN ME. SMACK

I DIDN'T EVEN KNOW THIS NEIGHBORHOOD EXISTED.
CHECK OUT ALL THE FRICKIN' MANSIONS.
JUST LOOKS LIKE YOUR HOOD TO ME.

HEY, I KNOW THAT GIRL. SHE GOES TO MY SCHOOL.
GOMEZ!
HI, TONTA!

WHATCHA DOIN'? YOU LIVE HERE?
UH-UH, I'M GOING TO HILLY JOHNSON'S HOUSE. WE HAVE TO MEET THE NEW P.E. COACH.

PARTAKING IN SPORTS THIS YEAR?
I GUESS SO. MY MOM'S MAKING ME. SHE SAID I HAVE TO EMBRACE MY HEALTH LIKE I DO MY COMICS.

YEAH? I WAS ON THE SWIM TEAM WITH HILLY MY FRESHMAN YEAR.
REALLY? SHE'S WAY LIKE, BRADBURY'S BEST ATHLETE! YOU GONNA COME SAY HELLO?
7.

NAH, I'M GOOD. YOU GO AHEAD, HAVE FUN WITH THE JOCK MAHONEYS.
AW, OK. WISH ME LUCK.

GO ON, TONTA. DON'T YOU WANNA SAY HI TO YOUR BFF TEAMMATE?
DON'T YOU WANNA SUCK ON YOUR OWN HUEVOS?

TONTA! COACH RIVERA WANTS TO TALK TO YOU!
?

SHE SAYS SHE KNOWS YOU.
I KNOW TONTA, ALL RIGHT.
LISTEN, THEY TELL ME YOU WERE ON THE SWIM TEAM YOUR FRESHMAN YEAR.
YEH.

DO YOU DO ANY OTHER SPORTS?
NO.
I WAS JUST TELLING THE GIRLS I WAS THINKING OF ADDING MORE SPORTS TO THE SCHOOL ROSTER.

WHAT DO YOU GIRLS THINK OF GYMNASTICS?
YEAH!
YES!
YEAH!
LACROSSE?
YES!
SURE!

RUGBY?
UH...
YES.
JUDO?
...
WRESTLING?
BOXING?
...

WELL, I'M DEFINITELY OPEN TO SUG-GESTIONS.
REMEMBER, TRYOUTS FOR VOLLEYBALL AND TENNIS START IN EARLY AUGUST.
OH, AND TONTA...
?

IT WOULD BE REALLY COOL IF YOU CAME OUT FOR SWIM OR ANY OF THE OTHER SPORTS THIS YEAR.
AND HERE'S MY NEW NUMBER IF YOU EVER WANT TO HANG OUT, CATCH UP ON THINGS. Y'KNOW...
K.

BOXING? JUDO? SOMETHING TELLS ME THIS IS GONNA BE A STRANGE YEAR.
WHY, THEY'RE REAL SPORTS.
WHAT DID SHE GIVE YOU?
NOTHIN'.

WHAT'S SHE LIKE, REALLY?
WHY ASK ME?
'CAUSE YOU KNOW HER.
NO, I DON'T.
WELL, SHE KNOWS YOU.
WELL, I DON'T KNOW HER.

ARE YOU GUYS LIKE, IN A BAND?
IT'S NOT A BAND, IT'S A GANG!
CAN I RIDE YOUR SKATE-BOARD?
SURE.
ME NEXT!

OH, GREAT MOVE, MOSES. NOW WE'LL NEVER GET OUT OF HERE.
YOU HAVE A NICE HOUSE, HILLY.
THANK YOU.

9.

THEY'RE WRONG, YOU KNOW. COACH IS WAY COOL. I'VE BEEN TO HER HOUSE.
YOU HAVE? WHAD YOU GUYS DO?
WE JUST WENT OVER THE SAME STUFF WE DID TODAY.

WHAT'S HER HOUSE LIKE? DOES SHE LIVE ALONE? DOES SHE HAVE A HUSBAND OR A BOYFRIEND, OR ...?
SHE LIVES WITH HER PARENTS IN TARZANA.
EW!

HEY, YOU'RE NOT GONNA TELL THOSE GIRLS WHAT I JUST SAID...
WHO, US TELL THEM ANYTHING?

WE SO GOTTA GET TO TARZANA.
WAY.

10.

WALABALOOOO...

WHO DARES CALL ON THE MYSTIC WATER SERPENT OF LEGUME LAGOON?
HEY, GRETCH.

THE NEW P.E. COACH AT BRADBURY? YES, I HEARD ABOUT HER.
WELL, SHE CLAIMS TO KNOW ME AN' SHE WANTS ME TO JOIN THE SWIM TEAM AN' STUFF...

YOU SHOULD JOIN. YOU'RE A GOOD SWIMMER.
I DUNNO, I'M STILL KINDA FREAKED OUT THAT SHE KNOWS ME. SHE DOESN'T KNOW ME!

YOU KNOW, YOU COULD JUST GO UP TO HER AND ASK HER BUT WHAT FUN WOULD THAT BE?
LET ME SEE THAT PHONE NUMBER SHE GAVE YOU.
YOU WANNA CRANK CALL HER?

WHAT DID SHE WRITE THIS ON?
IT'S A FLIER FOR SOME SORT OF SPORTING EVENT...
FIGURES.
HEY, WHAT'S THE LATEST ON OUR MYSTERIOUS FOREST SPIRIT?

I'M WEARING IT.
SHE LEFT YOU A BIKINI?
NO, MY NECKLACE. I FOUND IT HANGING ON A TREE BRANCH.

11.

MEDUSA?
SHE LEFT YOU ONE, TOO.

STUPID?! THANKS A LOT, FOREST SPIRIT MEDUSA!
YOU KNOW I WOULD NEVER CALL YOU THAT, TONTA.

IF YOU REMEMBER, THESE ARE THE SAME NAMES WE TALKED ABOUT THAT SAME FIRST DAY WE FOUND MANIC KINHEAD.
MEDUSA

WELL, I SURE AM NOT SAYING SHIT AROUND HERE ANY MORE.
YOU HEAR THAT, SPIRITY?
PERHAPS IF WE WHISPER LIKE SERPENTS...

THAT WAS DEFINITELY NOT HERE FIVE MINUTES AGO...
SHE CAN'T BE FAR.

YOU TAKE MANIC KINHEAD AND GO THAT WAY AND I'LL GO THIS WAY...
GO!

12.

ANYTHING?!
NOT YET!
HA HA!

KAIIIEEELEEEEE!

WORK IT, GIRL.
DON'T SPEAR ME.

SHE IS SLICKER THAN I THOUGHT.
YOU MEAN HE. THEY.
THE FOREST SPIRIT IS JUST TWO STONERS FRICKIN' AROUND.

STEVEN AND JORDAN? COULDN'T BE THEM.
THEY WERE THE ONLY ONES NEARBY BESIDES US, GRETCH.
I TUTORED THEM. THEY CAN BARELY SPELL THEIR OWN NAMES.

WHATEVS., I GOTTA GO. I'M STARVIN'.
WE CAN EAT BERRIES RIGHT OFF THE BUSH.
SHARE 'EM WITH THE FOREST SPIRIT.

13.

DON'T YOU WANT YOUR NECK-LACE?
NO, THANKS. THAT'S A RETURN ITEM FROM STOPID OL' ME.
I TRULY BELIEVE SHE MEANS NO DISRESPECT, TONTA! SHE'S PROBABLY JUST LONELY!
LET HER STAY LONELY! BYE!
!!
XAIME 13
14.

< SOMEWHERE OUTSIDE THE U.S. BORDER...

< IN THE TOWN OF PALOMAR...>

< KILLER RIVERA HAS RETURNED.>

SONG of our SAD GIRL

BETO/2013

GRAMPA AND GRANDMA CARMEN.
MY MOM.
PIPO.
AND WHO MIGHT THEY BE GOSSIPING ABOUT?

< THEY'VE BEEN TALKING ABOUT YOU BEHIND YOUR BACK AGAIN, DORA.>
< PRETEND I'M NOT HERE.>
< WE JUST WANT YOU TO BE HAPPY, DORA.>
< PAPA, IF SHE WANTS TO QUIT HER ACTING, SHE CAN.>
< WE ALL WANT WHAT'S BEST FOR YOU, KILLER.>

< I'M JUST BETTER AT BELLYDANCING THAN ACTING, IS ALL.>
< MOVIE AND TV CRITICS HAVE BEEN PRETTY HARD ON HER.
< HARSH, I MEAN HARSH ON HER.>

< KILLER, I TRAVEL FOR MY WORK, YOU TRAVEL FOR YOUR WORK.
< IT JUST WOULD NOT WORK.>

< DID I JUST SAY 'WORK' ENOUGH TIMES THERE?>

< I GUESS YOU'VE NEVER HEARD ABOUT LOVE.
< GOOD BYE.>
2

DR. BOCA

<YEAH, THEY TALKED ABOUT KILLER HAVING A BABY.
<DORALIS RIVERA IS KILLER'S REAL NAME.>

<SHE'LL BE FINE, PIPO.>
<I'LL BE RIGHT HERE, DORA.>

<WHAT?>
<FILM AND TV PRODUCER PIPO JIMENEZ ACCOMPANIED ACTRESS KILLER RIVERA TO A PRIVATE DOCTOR.>

<ON THE LATINO ENTERTAINMENT NEWS?>
<YEAH, THE NEWS OF YOU BEING PREGNANT HAS ALREADY BEEN LEAKED OUT.>

<THE CAB DRIVER, HUH?
<I HAVE TO REMEMBER NOT TO TALK ABOUT PERSONAL STUFF IN FRONT OF STRANGERS.
<THINK THE DOCTOR AND THE NURSE WILL RAT ME OUT ABOUT THE REST OF IT?>
3

THIS SCRIPT I'M WRITING ABOUT GRANDMA'S LIFE IS COMING TO ME PRETTY EASY.
I'M GLAD YOU'RE LEAVING OUT THE PART WHERE SHE DIES OF A BRAIN TUMOR, DORALIS.
AND WHERE SHE ABANDONS MOM AS A BABY.
AND WHEN...
GUADALUPE, PROMISE ME THAT IF YOU EVER HAVE A DAUGHTER, YOU'LL NAME HER AFTER ME.
WHY?
ARE YOU PLANNING ON DYING SOON?
YOU NEVER KNOW.
GRANDMA WASN'T TOO OLD WHEN SHE DIED.
HEY, YOU'RE SERIOUS.
DORALIS, GRANDMA HAD A BRAIN TUMOR CAUSED BY A HEAD INJURY.'
YOUR HEAD'S AS HARD AS A ROCK; YOU'LL END UP BURYING US ALL, SILLY.
OOH, THAT SOUNDS LIKE TOO MUCH WORK.
I THINK I'LL LIVE FOREVER INSTEAD.
ARE YOU ASHAMED OF ME; YOUR OWN SISTER?
OK, OK; I PROMISE IF I EVER HAVE A DAUGHTER...
CHECK THAT OFF MY TO DO LIST.

WRENCH WORLD
NOT FUCK SUMMER...
FUCK OOOT...
FUCK OOOOOOT...

ON OUR OWN TERMS...
ON OUR OWN TURDS...
FUCK OFF...

WOOOOOOOOOOOOOOO...
RRRRRRRRR
ULANC

???
OLICE

MOMMA, TONTA!

WHERE YOU BEEN, GIRL? YOUR SISTER'S BEEN TRYING TO CALL YOU.
MY MOM FLUSHED MY PHONE DOWN A BEMIS.
SOMEONE SHOT AL, YOUR STEP-DAD!
1.

HUH??
HE DIDN'T DIE BUT HE HAD TO GO TO THE HOSPITAL.
LOOKS LIKE A BURGLAR BROKE INTO YO' HOUSE AN' YO' DADDY SURPRISED HIM.

WHERE'S MY MOM?
DON'T WORRY, SHE WAS IN EL TORO WITH YOUR BABY BROTHER ALBY THIS WHOLE TIME.
WE CALLED'ER. SHE SAID FO' YOU GALS T' SIT TIGHT. SHE'S ON'ER WAY TO TH' HOSPITAL.

DON'T LET 'EM WAIT IN THEIR HOUSE, MOMMA.
OF COURSE NOT. YOU GIRLS COME WAIT AT OUR HOUSE.
IT WAS AL'S DAY OFF. HE WAS GONNA WATCH THE DODGERS.
THEY GOT A GOOD CHANCE THIS YEAR.

WHAT ARE YOU DOING OUT HERE?
WAITING FOR YOU, MOM.
WERE YOU AT THE HOSPITAL ALL NIGHT?

NO, I DECIDED TO GET A HOTEL ROOM. HAVE YOU HAD BREAKFAST?
NO.
NO.

2.

HMP.
YOU TWO LOOK LIKE A COUPLE OF STREET URCHINS.

MRS. CASTOR, IF I MAY ASK YOU JUST A FEW MORE QUESTIONS.
I TOLD YOU, I WAS IN EL TORO VISITING A FRIEND. WHAT ELSE IS THERE TO KNOW?

DID MR. CASTOR KNOW ANYONE WHO MIGHT WANT TO HARM HIM IN ANY WAY?
THERE'S NO CONSPIRACY! IT WAS HIS DAMN DAY OFF!
NOW, MAY I GO FINISH MY BREAKFAST WITH MY FAMILY?

WE'LL BE IN TOUCH.
NEXT TIME SEND DETECTIVE SLOBINSKI. HE KNOWS HOW TO TREAT PEOPLE LIKE HUMAN BEINGS.

AND NEXT TIME YOU TELL ME WHO'S AT THE DOOR BEFORE YOU GODDAMN ANSWER IT.

WHEN DO WE GET TO VISIT AL?

MOM, WHEN DO WE...?
THEY WILL LET US KNOW. IT'S STILL TOO EARLY TO...
WHAT IS THAT?
3.

WHAT IS WHAT?
THAT!
IT LOOKS LIKE BLOOD. I GUESS THEY MISSED A SPOT WHILE CLEANING UP.

YOU CAN'T COUNT ON ANY-BODY TO DO ANYTHING...
AND, WHERE'S MUÑECA?
UP IN HER ROOM. SHE'S STILL FREAKED OUT.

IS SHE SO FREAKED OUT, THAT SHE CAN'T EAT BREAKFAST WITH HER OWN FAMILY...?
SHE SAW THE BURGLAR TRYING TO KILL AL, MOM.

YOU WERE SUPPOSED TO BE AT THE MOVIES, MUÑECA! I GAVE YOU MONEY!
WE WERE AND THEN WE CAME HOME AND SAW AL ALL BLOODY AND...

IT'S JUST THAT YOU COULD HAVE GOT HURT, TOO.
THAT I COULD NOT HANDLE.

AND YOU COULDN'T GO WITH YOUR SISTER TO MAKE SURE SHE WAS SAFE? ONLY A MORON, TONTA...!

FUCK SUMMER.
XAIME 13
4.

WILLOW, WEEP NO MORE

by

BETO -2013-

< KILLER MADE THIS WITH YOUR HAMMER NEXT TO YOUR PICTURE, GRANDMA. >
JIMMY...!
< THAT'S SO CREATIVE, DORA. >

< I PUT THIS PICTURE OF GREAT GRANDMA NEXT TO YOURS. >
OK, GUYS; YOUR GRANDMA AND I'VE GOT TO GET GOING.

WE'LL TALK ABOUT THIS LATER, JIMMY.
HUH?

< YOU BE NICE TO MY GRANDSON, GUADALUPE. >
< JUST REMINDING HIM TO PAY ATTENTION, MAMA. >

I CAN'T BELIEVE YOU DID THAT, JIMMY!
WE DON'T KNOW HOW GRANDMA REALLY FEELS ABOUT HAVING BEEN ABANDONED BY GREAT GRAND-MA!
AW.
GRANDMA DOESN'T CARE, KILLER!

< HAVEN'T I MADE IT CLEAR TO EVERYONE THAT I COULDN'T CARE LESS ABOUT A MOTHER THAT I NEVER KNEW? >
< THAT'S RIGHT, MAMA.
< NEVER LOOK BACK. >

IT'S ADDRESSED TO MOM, KILLER, AND SHE SAID NOT TO CALL HER UNLESS IT'S FOR AN EMERGENCY.
TWIL
I BET MOM'LL CALL WHEN YOU'RE ON THE TOILET.
GUY, JIMMY!
MOMMM...
MOMMM... CALLLL...
P!NK
YEAH MOM, WE'RE FINE.
HEY, DO YOU THINK KILLER AND I COULD OPEN UP THE PACKAGE THAT YOUR TIA FRITZ SENT YOU?
OH, IT'S A SPECIAL DVD?
3

I HAF BEEN HEXPECTING YOU.
4

TELL ME D'TROOT, MEESTER BARNABAS: EET WASS YOU WHO MADE D'PHONE CALLS TO ME?
NO, BUT THAT'S WHAT I CAME TO TALK TO YOU ABOUT.
SO IMPORTANT DAT YOU BREAK EENTO MY HOME?
YOUR EX-HUSBAND MAY BE INVOLVED WITH THE PLUTONIUM THEFT.
I'D ADVISE YOU TO KEEP AWAY FROM HIM AND DON'T ANSWER THE PHONE.
CLICK

B··RING
`ALLO.
WASS WHO HERE? I DON' KNOW WHAT YOU TALK IT ABOUT!
WHO THEES EES?
THEES EES MY EX-HUSBAND, I BET IT!
BARNEY, I TELL YOU··
YOU KNOW WHO THIS IS.
YOUR FUTURE.
YOU TALK IT LIKE A CRAZY PERSON!
I GO NOW!
WE'LL TALK AGAIN SOON.
CLICK

BARNEY!
WHAT DID YOU TELL THEM ABOUT ME, HUH?
YOU TRASH!
YOU CAN'T THROW ME UNDER THE BUS!
I DON' GO ON NO BUS!
BARNEY, ESSTOP; I NO SAY NO TEENG!
YOWLP!

BARNEY!
I TELL YOU STAY AWAY, BUT NO!
VONDO..
VONDO.
YOU GIVE TO US D'SECRET PASSWORD NOW WHEN YOU ARE CHOKED TO DEATH?
WAIT, IS THAT IT?
JUST THIS ONE SCENE?
8

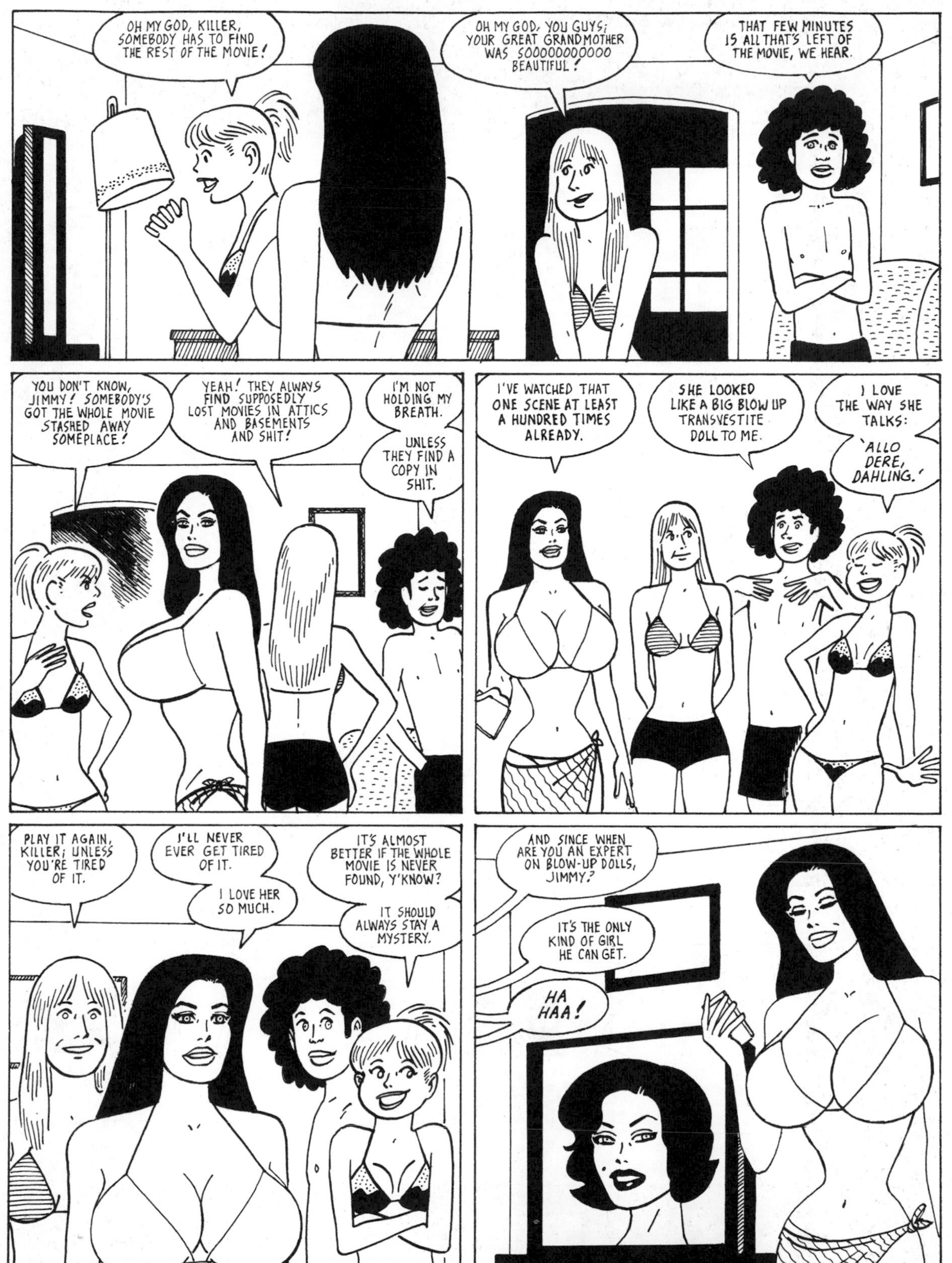
OH MY GOD, KILLER, SOMEBODY HAS TO FIND THE REST OF THE MOVIE!
OH MY GOD, YOU GUYS; YOUR GREAT GRANDMOTHER WAS SOOOOOOOOOOO BEAUTIFUL!
THAT FEW MINUTES IS ALL THAT'S LEFT OF THE MOVIE, WE HEAR.
YOU DON'T KNOW, JIMMY! SOMEBODY'S GOT THE WHOLE MOVIE STASHED AWAY SOMEPLACE!
YEAH! THEY ALWAYS FIND SUPPOSEDLY LOST MOVIES IN ATTICS AND BASEMENTS AND SHIT!
I'M NOT HOLDING MY BREATH.
UNLESS THEY FIND A COPY IN SHIT.
I'VE WATCHED THAT ONE SCENE AT LEAST A HUNDRED TIMES ALREADY.
SHE LOOKED LIKE A BIG BLOW UP TRANSVESTITE DOLL TO ME.
I LOVE THE WAY SHE TALKS:
'ALLO DERE, DAHLING.'
PLAY IT AGAIN, KILLER; UNLESS YOU'RE TIRED OF IT.
I'LL NEVER EVER GET TIRED OF IT.
I LOVE HER SO MUCH.
IT'S ALMOST BETTER IF THE WHOLE MOVIE IS NEVER FOUND, Y'KNOW?
IT SHOULD ALWAYS STAY A MYSTERY.
AND SINCE WHEN ARE YOU AN EXPERT ON BLOW-UP DOLLS, JIMMY?
IT'S THE ONLY KIND OF GIRL HE CAN GET.
HA HAA!
9

IF I WAS ALLOWED TO VOTE, THE OUTCOME WOULD'VE BEEN A LOT DIFFERENT, MARIA.
THANKS, KEVIN.
EES NOT LIKE I HOPE TO WIN NO ANYTIME.
MISS CHANNEL ISLANDS...
13
7
19
THEN WHY DO YOU CONTINUE TO ENTER THESE CONTESTS?
EXPOSURE!
HOLLYWOOD, SHE COULD USE A NEW ESTAR!
MARIA, WHO WAS LUBA?
YOU'VE BEEN REPEATING THAT NAME IN YOUR SLEEP AGAIN.
YOU CALL TO HER, LIKE SHE'S YOUR LONG LOST CHILD.
SHE CALLS TO ME, BUT I CAN'T SEE HER.
I CALL TO HER...
JUST-JUST A NIGHTMARES.
I DON' HAVE NO DAUGHTER AND I DON' KNOW NO LUBA.
MARIA, A MAN WANTS TO TALK TO YOU ABOUT YOU BEING IN A MOVIE!
13
9
13
9

CRIMEN
UNO

COBIA
CLU

ISH, WHAT'RE YA DOIN' HERE? AIN'T IT YER DAY OFF?
LEONARDO CALLED. SAID YOU NEEDED ME.

LEONARDO DON'T COME IN TODAY, NEITHER.
GUESS HE GOT YA, DAWG.
THAT'S NOT LIKE LEONARDO, THOUGH.

YOU YOUNG SKANKS DON'T KNOW JACKSHIT.
YOU AREN'T GOING TO GET ANYWHERE LAYING HERE LIKE SLICES OF BUTTERED TOAST.

WHEN I WAS SEVENTEEN, I WOULDA POLISHED OFF THREE RICH SUCKS AND STILL MADE VEGAS BEFORE NIGHTFALL.
IT'S ALL IN KNOWIN' AN' BLOWIN'.

ISH! BOY!
YOU CANCELLED YOUR DAY OFF JUST TO SEE ME?
VIOLET.

SIT WITH ME WHILE I FINISH MY DRINK.
WHERE'S VIVIAN?
VIVIAN'S NOT ALLOWED IN THE CLUB ANY MORE.
1.

SOUNDS LIKE THE SLUT.
GUESS IT'S JUST YOU AND ME.
HOW'D YOU KNOW IT'S MY DAY OFF?
YOU MADE LEONARDO CALL ME IN.
I NEEDED TO TALK TO YOU, ISH.
I WAS TAKING MY KIDS TO TRAVEL-TOWN TODAY!
WELL, DING DING, TOOT TOOT! THIS IS FUCKING IMPORTANT!
I TALKED TO MOM. SHE WANTS EVERYBODY TOGETHER FOR A FAMILY PORTRAIT.
THAT'S WHAT YOU NEEDED TO TELL ME?
I PROMISED HER I'D PASS IT ON TO ALL FAMILY MEMBERS, NO MATTER HOW PIGHEADED...
I'M OUTTA HERE.
SIT DOWN, ISH!
OK, GET THIS. SO, MY FRIEND JOLENA'S TELLING ME HOW SHE'S GOING DOWN ON THIS GUY SHE MET AT A PARTY AND HE'S BRAGGING HOW HE'S BEEN IN PRISON, KILLED PEOPLE...
SO, THEN I FIND OUT THIS GUY HAPPENS TO BE MY FUCKING EX-BOYFRIEND, THAT DIPSHIT THEY USED TO CALL BUNNY CHURRO...
PSYCHO DIPSHIT. GO ON...
SO, HE'S GOING ON AND THEN HE TELLS HER HE JUST GOT A JOB TO WHACK SOMEONE AND TELLS HER WHO AND EVERYTHING...
I'M AFRAID TO ASK BUT WHAT DOES THIS HAVE TO DO WITH ME?
IT HAS A LOT TO DO WITH YOU, ISH. A LOT TO DO WITH ALL OF US.
IT'S FAMILY, ISH.
XAIME 13
2.

Tarzana
ADVENTURES

CAR WASH! THIS WAY!
HELP OUR SCHOOL!
WOOOO!
Stop

HEY, THEY GOT A WAY BETTER CORNER THAN US, TONTA.
THEN WE BETTER GET ON IT.
FREE WAX JOB! WOOO!

HOW'S YOUR DAD...AL DOING?
SHOT TWICE IN THE HEAD, THROAT CUT FROM EAR TO EAR AND TODAY HE WAS WATCHING "FATHER KNOWS BEST."

THERE'S COACH RIVERA. OLD BITCH BETTER BE HAPPY I AGREED TO JOIN HER MICKIN' FRICKIN' SWIM TEAM.
DID I TELL YOU MY MOM STARTED TEACHING YOGA IN TARZANA, ONE BLOCK FROM COACH'S HOUSE?

THANKS FOR LETTING US COME ALONG, MOM.
YEAH, THANKS.
I'M GLAD TO HAVE YOU ALONG BUT THERE'S NOT MUCH TO DO HERE FOR TWO HOURS.

THAT'S COOL. WE JUST WANTED TO COME CHECK OUT TARZANA...
AND HERE IT IS...
DON'T STRAY TOO FAR.

SOMETIMES MY MOM IS SUCH A MOTHER.
MY MOM IS SUCH A MOTHER, TOO, BUT A WHOLE DIFFERENT KINDA MOTHER AND IT'S ALL THE FRICKIN' TIME.

TARZANA JUST LOOKS LIKE THE REST OF THE STUPID FRICKIN' VALLEY.
I KNOW, MY DAD MADE IT SOUND MUCH MORE SPECIAL 'CAUSE HE'S INTO EDGAR RICE BURROUGHS.
LIQUOR

HE'S INTO RICE BURROWS ???
YES, HE WROTE THE TARZAN BOOKS.
TARZAN...? TARZANA...?
I THOUGHT HIS WIFE'S NAME WAS JANE.
PEDOS Y POCHOS

MY DAD SAID MR. BURROUGHS IS BURIED HERE. NOT IN A CEMETERY BUT LIKE, IN SOME RANDOM COURTYARD ON VENTURA BOULEVARD.
MY DAD'S BURIED IN BELL GARDENS.

OH. SOMEONE'S THERE.
SO, WE'RE NOT DOING ANYTHING.

STARE ANY HARDER, WE'RE GONNA DISINTEGRATE.

TARZANA'S WEIRD. CAN WE GO BACK TO THE CAR, TONTA?
JUST WHEN WE'RE ABOUT TO HIT OUR DESIGNATED TARGET?

2.

IT'S A NICE HOUSE.
HOW DID YOU GET MISS RIVERA'S ADDRESS?
THE GORGON GOT IT FOR ME. THAT GIRL MAJORS IN SURVEILLANCE.

CAN WE HEAD BACK NOW? WE'VE BEEN STARING AT THAT HOUSE FOR OVER AN HOUR AND NOTHING'S HAPPENED.
WHY YOU SO ANXIOUS TO GET BACK? YOU MISS MOMMY?

I DON'T WANT HER TO WORRY IF SHE DOESN'T SEE US WHEN SHE COMES OUT.
SHE DIDN'T LOOK WORRIED TO ME WHEN SHE LEFT US. IF MY MOM TRUSTED ME LIKE THAT, I'D BE GONE LIKE A FRICKIN' SHOT.
DON'T PARK HERE

AREN'T YOU ALWAYS GONE LIKE A SHOT, ANYWAY?
YEAH, BUT WHEN MY MOM SENDS ME OFF, IT'S WITH A FRICKIN' STEELTOE UP MY POOPCHUTE. AT LEAST YOU HAVE YOUR MOM'S BLESSING. YOUR MOM'S WAY COOL.

YOUR MOM'S COOL, TOO, RIGHT, TONTA? YOU HAVE HER BLESSING, TOO, RIGHT...?
DO YOUR IRISES EVER TOUCH YOUR EYELIDS?

YOU AND STINKEYE BOY BACK THERE SHOULD HAVE A STARING CONTEST TO SEE WHO IGNITES FIRST.
OR WE COULD BOTH IGNITE YOUR POOPCHUTE!
XAIME '13

3.

URCHINS

¡MUÑECA!
WHAT ARE YOU GUYS DOING IN MY FRICKIN' ROOM? IN MY BED?
CAN WE SLEEP HERE TONIGHT?

WHY? WHERE'S MOM?
DID SHE GO SEE AL?
I DUNNO. SHE'S JUST OUT, AS USUAL.

SHE SAID I SHOULDN'T HAVE TOLD THE POLICE WHAT I SAW.
WHY? WERE YOU WEARING THE WRONG SHOES AT THE TIME?

SHE SAID IT WAS BECAUSE THE BURGLAR MIGHT COME BACK TO SILENCE ME.
DO YOU THINK THAT'S TRUE?
NAH.

DO YOU?
I DUNNO...

WHAT WAS THAT?
MOM, I THINK...

YEAH, SMELLS LIKE FAKE CHANEL.
IS SHE CRYING?
XAIME '13
1.

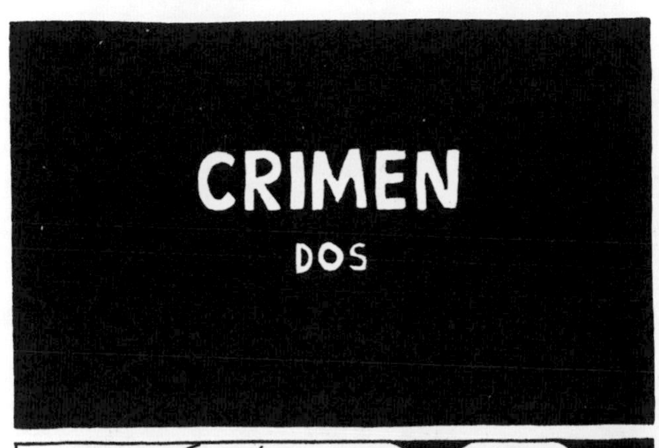
CRIMEN
DOS

CASTOR.
THE NAME DOES NOT RING A BELL.
I TOLD YOU, HE'S MOM'S LATEST HUSBAND.

WHACKED.
THAT'S FUCKED UP. WHA'D HE DO, OWE SOMEBODY MONEY?
BOAT INSURANCE SALESMAN.

YOU DIDN'T KNOW SHE WAS REMARRIED?
THE LAST ONE I KNEW ABOUT WAS HUSBAND NUMBER THREE, THE ARMENIAN GUY.

YOU'RE ONLY TWO BEHIND.
I GUESS YOU AND MOM STILL DON'T TALK...
SO?
SO, IT'S GOING ON LIKE, TWENTY YEARS...

THAT'S OUR BUSINESS, MINE AND MOM'S.
WELL, I THINK IT'S KIND OF MY BUSINESS, TOO, BEING A MEMBER OF THIS FAMILY.

IT WAS YOUR BUSINESS UNTIL THAT DAY YOU CHANGED YOUR STORY.
YOU HAVE TO ADMIT, THAT WAS A TOUGH POSITION FOR ME TO BE IN. WE WERE ACCUSING MOM OF SOME PRETTY SERIOUS SHIT.

IT WAS ALWAYS CLEAR TO ME.
SO, TWENTY YEARS LATER YOU STILL BELIEVE OUR MOTHER HAD SOMETHING TO DO WITH YOUR FATHER'S DEATH.

1.

EVEN AFTER EVERYBODY DECLARED IT AN ACCIDENT? THE POLICE, THE COURT, THE NEWS, MAURY POVICH...?
THAT DOESN'T CHANGE THE FACT THAT OUR MOM WAS INVOLVED.
BUT YOU DON'T THINK IT WAS AN ACCIDENT.
NEITHER DO YOU OR YOU WOULDN'T BE HERE.
SO, SAY IT AND GET IT OVER WITH...
I THINK WE CAN REALLY NAIL THE OLD BITCH THIS TIME.
THIS TIME I'M WITH YOU ALL THE WAY.
OOF.
ISH, I'M SERIOUS.
I BELIEVE YOU, BUT ARE YOU FUCKIN' SHITTING ME?
DROVE BY THEIR HOUSE YESTERDAY. IT MUST HAVE JUST GONE DOWN BECAUSE...
HOW DID YOU KNOW IT WOULD GO DOWN AT THE HOUSE? DID JOLENA TELL YOU THAT, TOO?
I TOOK A CHANCE.
LOOK, IF YOU THINK I HAD SOMETHING TO DO WITH THIS, SAY SO! I WANNA HELP YOU PUT MOM AWAY BUT I DIDN'T WANT THIS POOR SUCKER WHACKED TO HELP OUR CASE, EITHER!
YOU'RE ABSOLUTELY SURE MOM IS INVOLVED.
WIFE DID THE HIRING. NOT EX-WIFE OR MISTRESS. WIFE.
WIFE COULD MEAN EX-WIFE.
LOOK, WE CAN SIT ALL DAY AND PLAY DETECTIVE OR WE CAN LET REAL DETECTIVES DO IT.
I'M WILLING TO TAKE THE CHANCE OF BEING CALLED CRAZY, AT LEAST FOR OLD AL'S SAKE...
HOW ABOUT YOU, ISH?
XAIME '13
2.

..KILLER'S DAD
GRAMPA
HECTOR?

IT'S ON THE LATINO ENTERTAINMENT NEWS, HECTOR.
I'M LOOKING AT IT NOW!

BLACKIE CALLED TO TELL ME!
KILLER'S PREGNANT!

MY BABY'S GOING TO HAVE A BABY!

TOYS

<NEWS UPDATE.>
<DID KILLER RIVERA GO INTO HOSPITAL FOR MORE THAN JUST A PREGNANCY TEST?>

OH, HECTOR...

KILLER IN THE MIX

BETO 2013

HEY, GUADALUPE!
HEY, SANDY!
DORA'S GOING TO HAVE A FRIEND PICK HER UP, ALL RIGHT?
HAVE FUN!
SAD GIRL

GLAD TO BE BACK IN THE GOOD OL' USA, SANDY.
OH, I CAN SEE THAT YOU CAN BARELY HOLD IN YOUR GLEE.
SAD GIRL

BIG ANNIVERSARY DVD RE-RELEASE OF *MARIA M;* DIRECTOR'S CUT.
IT WAS DURING THE MAKING OF THIS MOVIE WHEN FRITZ HAD FINALLY LOST ALL HER MARBLES.
TSK, DAD.

INTERESTING TO HEAR THAT YOU'LL PUT YOUR TALENTS INTO YOUR BELLYDANCING MORE THAN YOUR ACTING NOW, KILLER.
SAD GIRL

BUT IF THOSE GRADES AREN'T UP SOON, NO MORE BELLYDANCING.
MOM'S GOT A BIG MOUTH.

SHE ALSO TOLD ME THAT YOU'RE NOT SO NICE TO THE NICE BOYS THAT ASK YOU OUT, KILLER.
JUST BECAUSE I DON'T SAY YES, THAT DOESN'T MAKE ME MEAN OR ANYTHING, DAD.

WELL, COULD YOU SAY NO A FEW MORE TIMES TO THE ASSHOLE PRICKS THAT USE YOU, PLEASE?
SO YOU AND MOM ARE THE BIG EXPERTS ON MY LIFE NOW?
GUY, DAD; GIVE ME SOME CREDIT.

SPOKEN LIKE A TRUE FUTURE CHILDLESS SPINSTER.
JUST BRING THOSE GRADES UP BECAUSE YOU'RE GOING TO NEED SOME BRAINS TO SURVIVE WHEN THERE'S NOBODY LEFT TO DUMP YOU.
2

PEACH
SAD GIRL
SO DID YOU TOTALLY QUIT BELLYDANCING OR WHAT?
NOT ALL OF US HAVE A TEENY TINY SERPENTINE WAIST, KILLER.
SAD GIRL
MOST PEOPLE CALL IT MY FREAKISH SERPENTINE WAIST, SANDY.
TYPICAL JEALOUS CRAP.
OH, WHEN WE THOUGHT THAT I WAS PREGNANT, YOUR DAD WANTED ME TO STOP DANCING FOR A WHILE.
NOW THAT WE KNOW I'M NOT...
SAD GIRL
YOUR DAD'S JUST WORRIED THAT YOU'LL END UP A TRAIN WRECK LIKE FRITZ.
PERSONALLY, I THINK FRITZ IS AWESOME BUT YOUR DAD'S JUST BEING A DAD.
WAS THAT TEDDY BEAR FOR THE BABY?
HE RAN OUT AND BOUGHT IT AS SOON AS HE HEARD YOU WERE PREGNANT.
HE'LL GET OVER IT IN TIME, KILLER.
LUCKY HIM.
SAD GIRL
3

PEACH

OH, NOTHING'S UP, OTHER THAN I'M A FUTURE CHILDLESS SPINSTER AND MY DAD DOESN'T LOVE ME.
KILLER, IT'S YOUR BODY!
AND HIS GRANDKID.
WOULD'VE BEEN.

GUY...
HELLO?

DAD..?
OH...

OK.
YEAH, OK! LUNCH WOULD BE GREAT!
SEE YOU THERE!
4

< I LEFT MY BABY.
< HOW CAN I BE FORGIVEN?
< GOD FORGIVES, MARIA.>
< I COULDN'T TAKE CARE OF HER.
< SHE WAS BETTER OFF BEING RAISED BY OTHERS.>
< YES, MARIA.>
< MAYBE SHE'LL GROW UP TO BE RICH OR FAMOUS, HUH?
< LIKE A MOVIE STAR OR SOMETHING.>
< ANYTHING'S POSSIBLE.>
SALE 20% OFF
< HEY, I WAS OFFERED A NEW MOVIE, BUT I TURNED IT DOWN FLAT!
< THAT ONE MOVIE I MADE YEARS AGO WAS SO BAD THAT IT HARDLY PLAYED ANYWHERE, I HEAR.
< NEVER AGAIN.>
< OUR LOSS.>
YEAH...
< LOSS.>
SIGH
< MAYBE I'LL BE FORGIVEN SOMEDAY.>
AHHH...
< I KNOW LUBA HAD A BETTER LIFE WITHOUT ME.
< HAS A BETTER LIFE.
< WHEREVER SHE IS.>

CRIMEN
TRES

I TALKED TO JOLENA.
SHE DENIED EVERYTHING.
TO A TEE.

VIVIAN SAYS SHE'S IN.
SHE SHOULD BE HERE ANY MINUTE.
THE MORE THE MERRIER, I GUESS.

HE WASN'T ONLY YOUR DAD, ISH. IT HIT HER JUST AS HARD.
"SHAKES THE CLOWN."
WHAT?

THAT'S THE MOVIE I WAS TRYING TO REMEMBER. IT WAS THE ONE MOM SENT US TO ON THE DAY OF THE "ACCIDENT."
YOU DON'T HAVE TO TELL ME, ISH. I PICKED THAT ATROCITY.

I BEGGED AND BEGGED TO GO SEE IT BECAUSE IT HAD A FUCKING CLOWN IN IT.
MOM WANTED US TO SEE "HOME ALONE 2."
I WANTED TO SEE "MIGHTY DUCKS."

WHAT ARE WE DOING?
THE RIGHT THING. NOW, STOP...
VIVIAN!
VIOLET, WHA'D YOU DO TO YOUR HAIR?

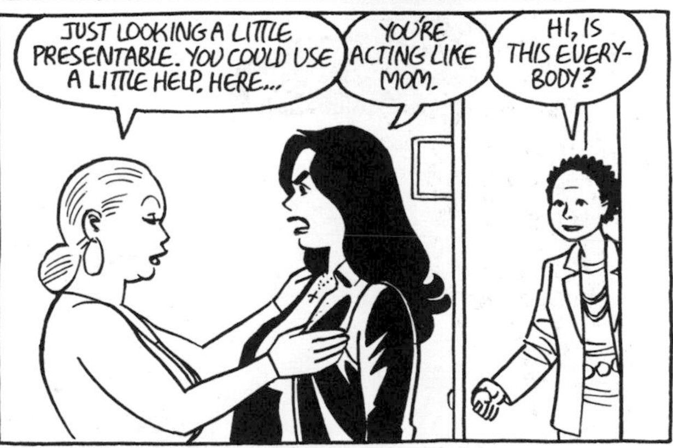
JUST LOOKING A LITTLE PRESENTABLE. YOU COULD USE A LITTLE HELP, HERE...
YOU'RE ACTING LIKE MOM.
HI, IS THIS EVERY-BODY?
1.

THANKS FOR JOINING US, VIVIAN.
WHO SAID I'M DOING IT FOR YOU?
YOU GUYS STOP IT.
SO, IT IS OUR BELIEF, ISH'S, VIVIAN'S AND MINE THAT OUR MOTHER HIRED THE SUSPECT TO KILL HER HUSBAND BUT TO MAKE IT SEEM LIKE A BOTCHED BURGLARY.
SAME AS YOU BELIEVE SHE WAS DIRECTLY INVOLVED IN THE ACCIDENT THAT KILLED ISH'S AND VIVIAN'S FATHER TWENTY YEARS AGO...
YES.
YES.
WELL, THIS DEFINITELY OPENS THINGS UP. I'M GOING TO HAVE TO HAVE YOU COME IN AND INTERVIEW YOU INDIVIDUALLY.
FINE.
DO I HAVE TO DO IT?
WE'RE GOING TO NEED YOUR TESTIMONY, VIVIAN...
HOW THE FUCK CAN I REMEMBER SHIT THAT HAPPENED TWENTY YEARS AGO?
YOU SAID YOU WERE GOING WITH US ALL THE WAY IN THIS, VIVIAN!
I DIDN'T THINK IT WOULD TAKE ALL THIS BULLSHIT GOING TO COURT AND SHIT...
YOU FUCKIN' SLUT, I HAVEN'T KICKED YOUR PUNKASS IN A LONG TIME...
THEN LET'S GO, BITCH...
GIRLS...
ISH...?
THEY GOT IT UNDER CONTROL.
XAIME 13
2.

PACK MULES

SO...

SO, IF YOU TAKE US, YOU CAN JUST DROP US OFF AND...
...AND WE CAN FIND A RIDE BACK AND...

HUH??
TO ANAHEIM. YOU DON'T HAVE TO STICK AROUND. WE CAN FIND A RIDE BACK...

I DUNNO, TONTA. ANAHEIM'S KINDA FAR AN' I GOT A LOTTA SHIT TO DO...
IT'S NOT LIKE I ASK YOU FOR STUFF EVERYDAY, FRANK LOPEZ.

IDIOT.
ASS.
BOOB.
I GUESS HE'S NOT GONNA TAKE US?

NO, BUT I SNAKED HIS KEYS. HERE, YOU DRIVE.
I DON'T WANNA TAKE PART IN ANY PILFERAGE...
YOU GOT THE DRIVER'S PERMIT, NOW, GET IN.

EEEE!
HERE HE COMES! WHAT DO I DO??
FLOOR IT!
I'LL DEAL WITH HIM LATER!

1.

ANAHEIM IS FAR, TONTA.
IT'D BE CLOSER IF YOU DROVE OVER 40, GOMEZ.
I'VE NEVER DRIVEN ON THE FREEWAY.

IS THIS RIGHT? IT'S AN INDOOR SWAP-MEET.
THAT'S WHAT THE INSTRUCTIONS SAY...
GO IN AND THROUGH TO THE REAR DOORS WITH SCRATCHED UP GLASS...
SUPER BARGAIN

LOOK, SCRATCHED UP GLASS.
THEN WE'RE SUPPOSED TO PUT ON THE MASKS INCLUDED IN THE MYSTERIOUS BLACK BAG.

FEELS LIKE WE'RE BEING INITIATED INTO SOME SECRET CULT.
THEN WE PAY WITH THE TWENTY DOLLAR BILL ALSO INCLUDED IN THE BLACK BAG.
THEN WHAT?
THEN WE GO IN. OUT.
$10

THIZ MUZZ BE DA PLAZE.
2.

WE DON'T HAVE TO WRESTLE, DO WE?
HOW SHOULD I KNOW? I CAN'T EVEN SEE.

THAT MUST HAVE BEEN BOMBERO INFANTIL AND MINI ELVIS VERSUS BIGOTE AZUL AND MONSTER BOY.
OK, BUT WHERE IS...?

GRETCHEN?
"LA MEDUSA ARBOLADA" IF YOU PLEASE. SIT, YOU'RE JUST IN TIME.

NICE TO MEET YOU AGAIN. YOU TUTORED ME ONCE.
I REMEMBER. YOU ASKED TONS OF QUESTIONS, HENCE YOUR LUCHADORA NAME, "LA INTERROGADORA INDOMABLE."

I CAN'T SEE. CAN I TAKE MINE OFF?
IT'S TOTALLY NECESSARY TO REMAIN INCOGNITO AT THIS TIME, "CIEGA NEGRA."

DAMAS Y CABALLEROS... LA CAMPEÓNA DESEA HACER...
WHAT'S HER FRICKIN' TRIP?

I WISH MY SPANISH WAS BETTER.
ALLOW ME TO TRANSLATE FOR YOU.
THAT WOMAN THROWING ATTITUDE IS DONNIE BROOKS. SHE'S THE WOMEN'S CHAMPION.
3.

DONNIE WANTS TO MAKE AN ANNOUNCEMENT TO HER CHALLENGER WHO HAS YET TO MAKE HER ENTRANCE. FOR SECURITY MEASURES, DONNIE IS BACKED BY THE ROXIDENTALS.

UH, GRETCH. THE GIRL IS SPEAKING IN CLEAR ENGLISH, THANK YOU.
YES, BUT WHAT YOU DON'T KNOW IS SHE'S DATING SHANE OF THE ROXIDENTALS WHO ONCE DATED HER CHALLENGER.
HERE COMES HER CHALLENGER NOW...

LA TERRORISTA DE EL PASO... LA MAGNIFICA...
ANGEL LA ASESINAAAA!

OH, MY GOD! COACH RIVERA IN THE FLESH!
YOW! NO WONDER WE'RE INCOGNITO!
THE ROXIDENTALS MIGHT NOT BE ENOUGH TO HOLD BACK THE ANGEL OF ALL ASSASSINS.

DONNIE'S ANNOUNCEMENT IS THAT SHE INJURED HER ARM YESTERDAY AND CAN'T DEFEND HER TITLE AGAINST ANGEL TODAY SO SHE'S OFFERING THAT SHANE TAKES HER PLACE. WHAT A BURN SINCE SHANO DUMPED ANGEL FOR THE CHAMPION.
4.

THE LAST FIVE OR SIX YEARS OF MY LIFE HAVE BEEN QUITE LIFE ALTERING. I WENT OFF TO SCHOOL IN TEXAS BUT I WAS STILL STUCK ON MIKEY VARAN BACK HOME AND BY SOME MIRACLE I CONVINCED HIM TO FOLLOW ME.

I HAD NO IDEA WHAT I WAS DOING AND, I SUSPECT, NEITHER DID MIKEY. WE HAD THIS WEIRD NOT-GOING-ALL-THE-WAY-BOY/GIRLFRIEND-NOT-BOY/GIRLFRIEND RELATIONSHIP THAT SORT OF JUST FLOATED THERE IN LIMBO.

WHILE I DID MY SCHOOL THING, MIKEY GOT A JOB AT A MUSIC STORE AND JOINED A BAND. I WAS HAPPY THAT HE FOUND A REASON TO STICK AROUND THOUGH I WAS TOTALLY CLUELESS HOW TO FILL MY END.

HE STARTED TO GET CLOSE TO HIS LEAD SINGER. SHE WAS EVERYTHING I WASN'T. CONFIDENT, OUTGOING, EXPERIENCED. SHE STEPPED IN, STOLE MIKEY'S HEART AND STOMPED ON MINE. IT ALL HAPPENED SO FAST.

WHEN I TRIED TO FIGHT FOR WHAT I THOUGHT WAS MINE, MIKEY TURNED ON ME AND USED MY HALFWAY ROMANCING AS HIS REASON TO LEAVE. I WAS WAY TOO NAIVE TO REALIZE THAT SEX WOULD HAVE KEPT HIM HOME NIGHTS.

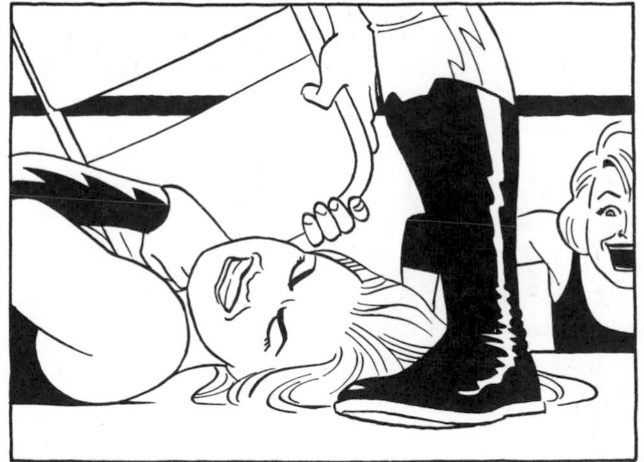

NOW WE BOTH KNOW WE SHOULD HAVE NEVER BEEN TOGETHER IN THE FIRST PLACE, BUT AT THE TIME I WAS FLOORED. I SUFFERED MY FIRST HEART-WRENCHING DUMPING WHERE MOST KIDS HAVE THEM YEARS EARLIER.

LUCKILY, MY FRIEND MAGGIE'S TEXAS RELATIVES AND FRIENDS WERE THERE TO CUSHION THE BLOW. THEY TOOK ME IN AS ONE OF THEIR OWN. INTRODUCED ME TO A WHOLE NEW TYPE OF RECREATIONAL ACTIVITY.

AFTER I GRADUATED I CAME HOME TO SO CAL. I'M REUNITED WITH MY FAMILY AND I'M LOOKING FORWARD TO MY NEW JOB AS P.E. TEACHER AT BRADBURY GIRLS' SCHOOL. BEYOND THAT IS ANYONE'S GUESS.

THAT WAS SO HEARTBREAKING! POOR MISS RIVERA GOT ROOKED!
MISS RIVERA GOT ROOKED AND ROCKED!
IF THAT'S WHAT P.E. IS GOING TO BE LIKE THIS YEAR, I'M TOTALLY IN.

NOW, YOU GIRLS KNOW WE CAN'T TELL ANYONE AT SCHOOL ABOUT THIS.
WHY NOT?
THIS IS MISS RIVERA'S PRIVATE LIFE, WHERE SHE GETS TO MOONLIGHT UNDER A SECRET ALTER EGO.
GATAS

WOULDN'T IT BE COOL TO LEAD A SECRET DOUBLE LIFE?
I WANTED TO BE BABY BOP WHEN I WAS LITTLE.

STUDENT BY DAY...
...FOREST SPIRIT BY NIGHT?
HEH HEH...

FOREST SPIRIT?
LA MEDUSA BLABLABLABA WILL FILL YOU IN. I GOTTA GO PEE.
XAIME 13

6.

CRESTFALLEN ANGEL

1.

WAIT! SO, HOW LATE ARE YOU GOING TO BE OUT?
I DUNNO, WHENEVER...
I'M JUST ASKING BECAUSE I HAVE TO GET UP PRETTY EARLY TOMORROW SO, IF THERE'S A LOT OF BANDS...
I CAN LET THEM GO AND WE CAN DO SOMETHING.
WELL, SURE... OK...
IT'S YOUR TOWN. WHAT DO YOU LIKE TO DO?
WELL, I'M NOT FROM THIS TOWN EXACTLY BUT...
I DON'T REALLY DO ANYTHING. I'M NOT A TEACHER YET, SO...
I'M SURE WE CAN FIND A QUIET BAR...
BUT YOU DON'T DRINK...
NO, SO...
WE CAN JUST GET COFFEE.
OH, I'D BE UP ALL NIGHT AND I GOTTA... SO...
OK...
WELL, THEY'RE CALLING, SO...
SEE YOU IN VANCOUVER! HA HA!
XAIME '13
2.

CRIMEN
CUATRO

WHAT NOW?
WE WAIT FOR THEIR CALL, I GUESS...
WHATEVER WHATEVS YOU. I'M GONE.

WAIT, VIVIAN. BEFORE YOU GO...
WE KNOW YOU'RE NOT GONNA TESTIFY, BUT ARE YOU STILL WITH US, AT LEAST?
CLARO.
REALLY, VIV...?

FUCK YEAH! FUCK MOM, FUCK CHURRO, FUCK MEL SPROPP...
VIVIAN, WE CAN'T BE SURE SPROPP IS INVOLVED, JUST BECAUSE HE AND MOM ARE OLD PALS.

WHATEVER. JUST 'CAUSE YOU'RE HIS FAITHFUL WHIPPING BOY...
NOW, WAIT...
TOOODLEE
HOLD ON, GUYS.

HELLO?
MOM...?
HO!

THAT WAS WEIRD TIMING.
WEIRD...
GUYS, AL DIDN'T MAKE IT.
1.

WAS SHE PRETENDING TO BE SAD?
ARE YOU GUYS PRETENDING YOU'RE SAD?
VIVIAN, PLEASE...
THOSE POOR KIDS...

WHEN HAVE YOU EVER CARED ABOUT "THOSE POOR KIDS?" WHEN HAVE YOU CARED ABOUT ANYBODY IN YOUR FAMILY, ISH?
I...
THAT'S NOT FAIR, VIVI...

I WAS TAKING MY KIDS TO TRAVELTOWN! I DIDN'T WANNA FALL INTO THIS BULLSHIT!
YEAH? SAW THEIR MOM THROWING CHANCLA AT LOS GLOBOS ON SUNSET.
VIVI...

I WAS THIS CLOSE TO FORGIVING MOM AFTER ALL THESE YEARS AND THEN
BANG!
YOUR WIFE MIGHTA STUCK AROUND IF YOU LET HER JUERGA VERGA ONCE IN AWHILE.
STOP...

I USED TO LAY AWAKE AT NIGHT WISHING THE BLUE FAIRY WOULD COME THROUGH MY WINDOW, TAP MY HEAD WITH HER WAND AND TELL ME DAD'S DEATH TRULY WAS AN ACCIDENT, THAT OUR MOTHER TRULY WAS FUCKING INNOCENT!

AW, THE BLUE FAIRY STORY...
I USED TO LAY AWAKE AT NIGHT WISHING MOM WOULD GET RAN OVER BY A STEAMROLLER.

NOWADAYS THAT WOULD BE A STEAMPUNKROLLER, RIGHT?
HAH?
I LOVE MY FUCKING FAMILY...

TO AL.
FUCK MOM.
TO DAD.
FUCK MOM.
TO ME.
FUCK ALL OF YOU.
XAIME 13

2.

I'VE HAD SO MANY FACES, BUT I REMEMBER THEM ALL.

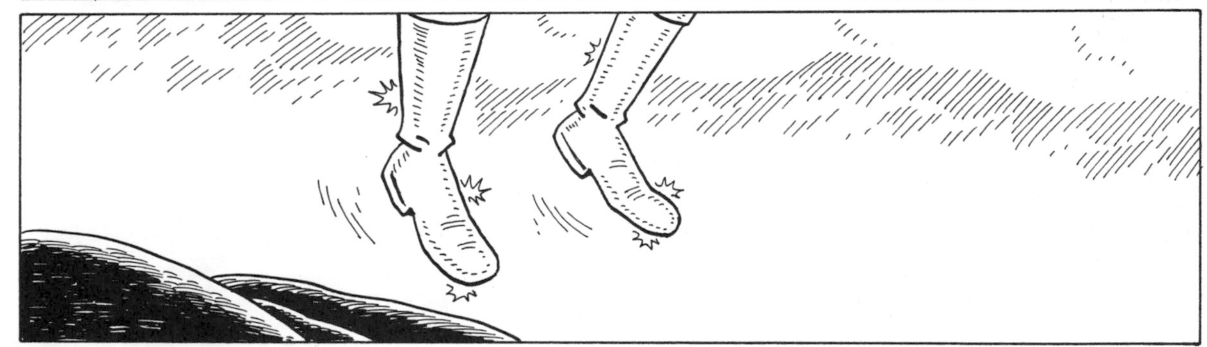

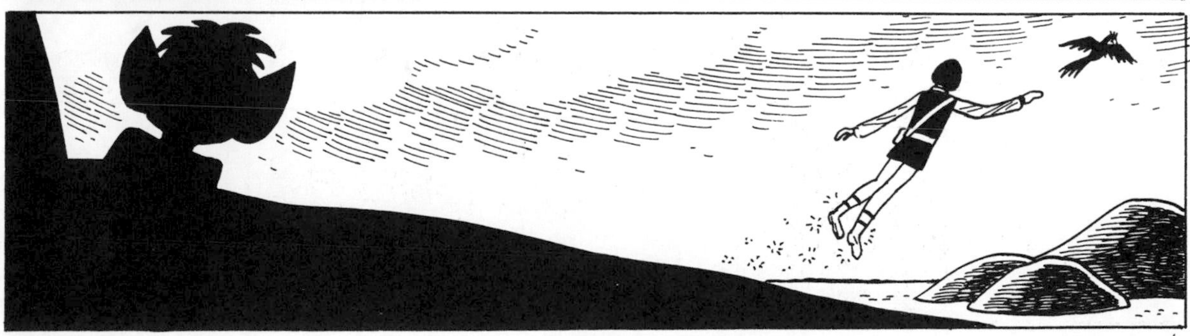

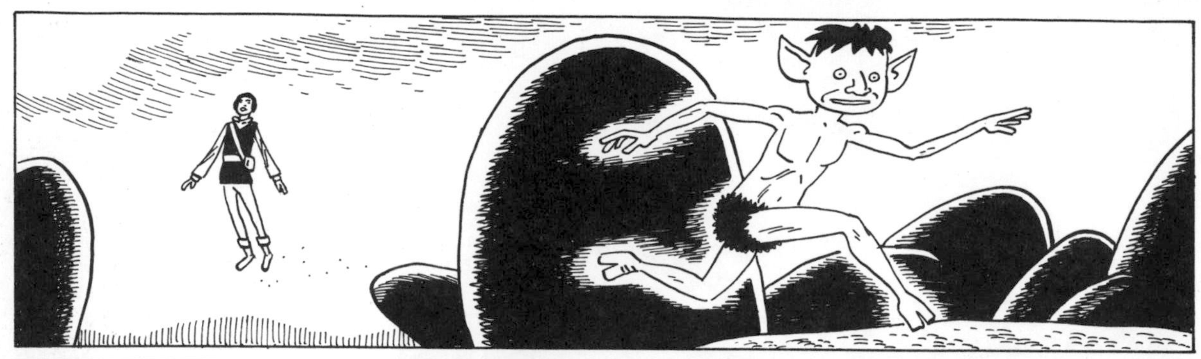

WHO THE FUCKING HELL DISTURBS MY MIDDAY MEAL?

A MORTAL FLIES THROUGH THE AIR WITH GLOWING BOOTS!
NO FUCKING SHIT?

I'LL CHECK THIS SHIT OUT MYSELF, BECAUSE IF YOU'RE MISTAKEN, I'LL FUCKING EAT YOU NEXT!

2

FUCKING SHIT ON A STICK, IT'S TRUE!
FUCKING BOOTS THAT CAN MAKE YOU FLY!

I'VE GOT TOTALLY AWESOME ABILITIES, BUT FLYING ISN'T ONE OF THEM.
WELL, THAT'S FUCKING ABOUT TO CHANGE!

A MAN THAT CAN FLY AND SO HANDSOME, TOO!

AH, FAIR FURRY.
IF YOU'RE AFTER MY MAGIC BOOTS, YOU'RE SHIT OUT OF LUCK.
WE'LL SEE ABOUT THAT, FARTFUCK.

3

4

DUMBFUCK DIDN'T KNOW WHO HE WAS DEALING WITH!
SLURRRRP!
DEAR GOD...
HE'S ALL YOURS, LITTLE SHIT FUCKERS, BUT DON'T TRASH THE BOOTS!
HE LOOKS STUPID DYING HIS HORRIBLE DEATH.
EEAAIII!!
YUM.
EASY FIT?
THEY'RE CHEAPLY MADE, BUT LOOKS AREN'T EVERYTHING.
IT'S PERFORMANCE WHAT COUNTS!

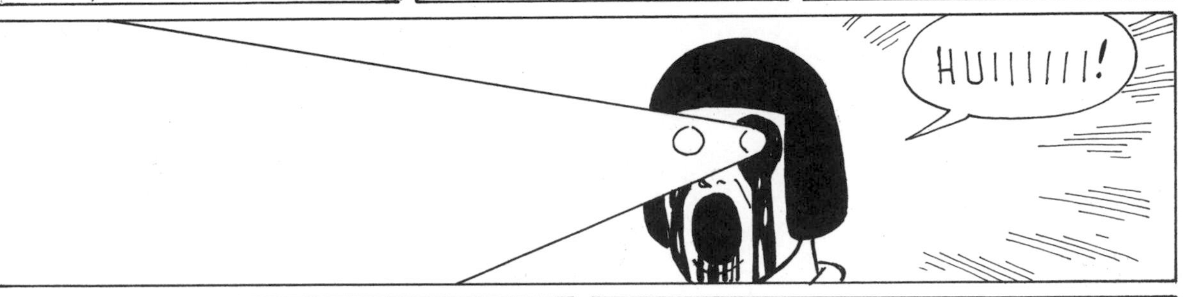

6

WELL.
THAT WORKED OUT BETTER THAN EXPECTED.
SLURP.

HEE.
NOW I CAN RESUME MY MISSION TO RID THE WORLD OF FUCKING COUNTRY MUSIC!

HA HAA!
NOBODY WILL KNOW WHY ONLY I CAN WEAR THE MAGIC BOOTS!

7

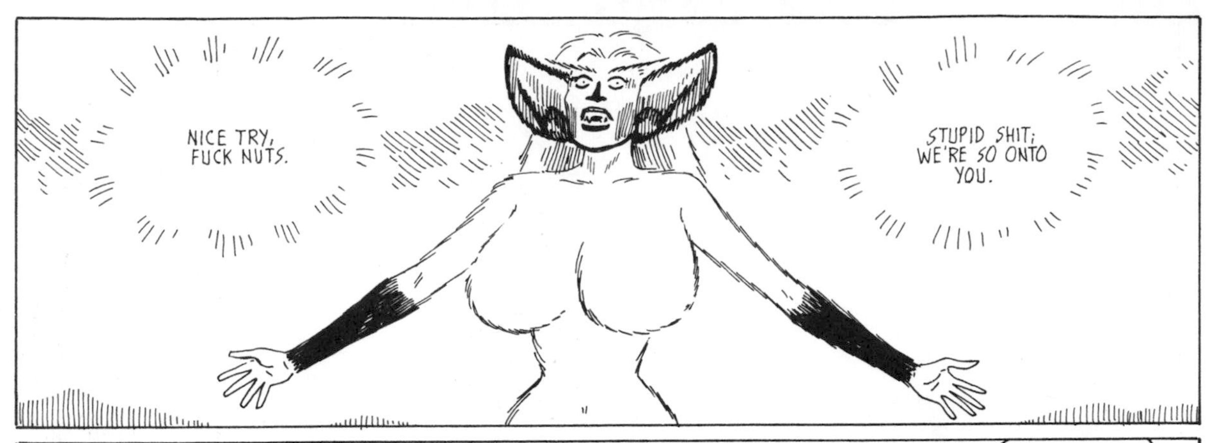
NICE TRY, FUCK NUTS.
STUPID SHIT; WE'RE SO ONTO YOU.

THE BOOTS WON'T GET YOU OUT OF THIS, DICKHOLE!
AND YOU CAN'T HIDE FROM US IN THAT UGLY-ASS BODY.

ONLY ONE OF OUR KIND CAN WEAR THE BOOTS, SO OF COURSE WE KNEW IT WAS YOU, MORON.

SENDING MAGIC BOOTS BACK UP TO MOTHERSHIP.
OVER.
ROGER THAT.
OVER.

8

HE-HE USED ME, THE FUCKING BASTARD, HE··
ASSWIPE'S PLAN FAILED SO I WOULDN'T SWEAT IT, BLIMPTITS.

HOW DO I KNOW YOU WON'T DO THE SAME?
YOU'RE NOT WORTH THE SHIT IN YOUR ASS, PIG BARF.
HA HA!

NIAGARA FALLS!
SLOWLY I TURNED, STEP BY STEP!

PWOP!

BACK TO THE MOTHERSHIP, FAILURE.
FUCK ALL OF Y'ALL!

HA HA HAAAA!

WHAT HAPPENED?
WHERE IS THE LOVE WE ONCE KNEW?

I'LL HAVE TO FIGURE OUT A DIFFERENT WAY TO RID THE WORLD OF COUNTRY MUSIC.

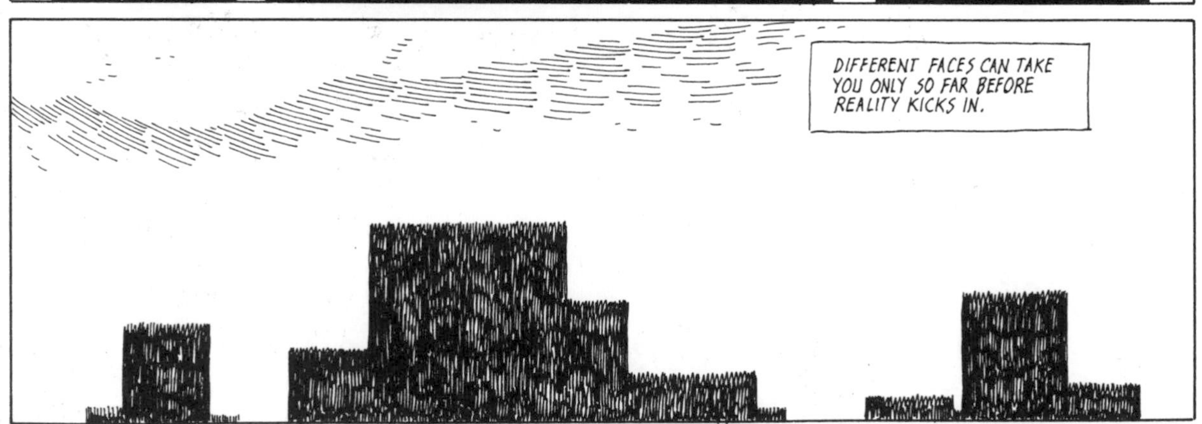
DIFFERENT FACES CAN TAKE YOU ONLY SO FAR BEFORE REALITY KICKS IN.

10

FAMILYLIMAF

OK, BEFORE YOU START YOUR FINAL LAPS, I NEED TWO VOLUNTEERS TO MOVE SOME TABLES AND CHAIRS FOR ME.

AND THERE ARE MY VOLUNTEERS RIGHT THERE...

APODACA
AGAGANIAN
GOMEZ
HOO
JOHNSON
ABZEKK

1.

AND TRY NOT TO HIT EACH OTHER OVER THE HEAD WITH THE CHAIRS OR EXECUTE ANY POWERBOMBS THROUGH THE TABLES.
?!?
BRADBURY

OH MY GOD, GOMEZ! SHE KNOWS WE WERE SPYING ON HER!
I GUESS WE WEREN'T INCOGNITO ENOUGH.
AT LEAST WE DON'T HAVE TO DO MORE LAPS.
GOMEZ

STILL IT'S NOT FAIR AN' I'M TELLING HER SO.
SHE'S BEEN SPYING ON US, TOO! HOW ELSE CAN SHE KNOW ME AN' I DON'T KNOW HER!
AGAJANIAN

?

VIVI??
WHAT ARE YOU DOING HE--?
JUST A SEC...

!?!

2.

FEEL LIKE OLD TIMES, ANGEL BABY?
VIVIAN!
WHAT THE HELL ARE YOU DOING?
BRADBURY
AGAJANIAN

OH MY GOD, I HOPE YOU'RE OLD FRIENDS.
IF YOU WANNA CALL IT THAT.
YOU GOTTA ADMIT, I HAD YOU TAPPING OUT.
BRAD BURY

OK, SHOW'S OVER! HIT THE SHOWERS!
THE BELL HASN'T RUNG.
RING!
THERE IT IS, NOW GO!
PINGLE

YOU KNOW, YOU'RE NOT SUPPOSED TO BE ON CAMPUS WITHOUT PERMISSION FROM THE FRONT OFFICE.
WE WERE ON OUR WAY TO GET PERMISSION TO PICK UP OUR SISTER UNTIL THIS MORON DECIDED TO RUN AMOK.

MY SISTER IS SO FRICKIN' MENTAL.
AT LEAST WE NOW KNOW HOW MISS RIVERA KNOWS YOU, TONTA.

TONTA!
SEE YOU LATER IN MATH... MAYBE!

IN A FEW MINUTES I'M GOING TO GET A NOTE FROM THE OFFICE FOR YOU TO LEAVE SCHOOL FOR THE DAY TO GO HOME WITH YOUR SISTERS...
WHY?
AGAJANIAN

3.

I ALSO WANTED TO TELL YOU HOW SORRY I AM ABOUT YOUR STEP-FATHER. YOUR SISTERS JUST TOLD ME AND... WELL, I'M SORRY.
THAT'S OK. WE WERE KINDA EXPECTING IT.
I DON'T KNOW IF YOU REMEMBER, BUT I WAS AT YOUR FATHER'S FUNERAL.
REALLY? YOU KNEW VIVI WAY BACK THEN?
BRADBURY
NO, ACTUALLY HIS RESTAURANT USED TO SPONSOR OUR SOFT-BALL TEAM.
HEY, I USED TO GO TO THOSE GAMES.
OF COURSE. YOU WERE OUR LOUDEST CHEER-LEADER.
THAT RESTAURANT WASN'T AROUND LONG. MOM BLAMED IT ON THE SIGN.
I GUESS "HARUT'S THAI PALACE" WASN'T THE BEST CATCH.
NOTE FOR YOU, MISS RIVERA.
BRADBUR
GO AHEAD AND GET DRESSED, TONTA. THEY'RE WAITING FOR YOU AT THE OFFICE.
WHY ARE THEY PICKING ME UP?
THEY'LL TELL YOU, NOW GO...
SHOWERS
MISS RIVERA...?
IS EVERYTHING ALL RIGHT?
SHOWERS
BURY
XAIME 13
4.

CRIMEN

CINCO

WE'RE NOT GOING TO THE COBIA CLUB, ARE WE? THAT PLACE IS EVIL AND THAT CREEP WORKS FOR THEM!
HE'S ALSO YOUR SUCKING BROTHER, NOW SHUT THE HELL FUCKING UP!
HUH...?
YOU DIDN'T KNOW, TONTA? GAW, HE'S ONLY VIVIAN'S TWIN.
NOT BY CHOICE.
NOBODY TELLS ME ANYTHING! I'M ALWAYS THE LAST TO KNOW!
WELL, YOU ALWAYS WANNA BE A LONER.
YEAH, REBEL GRLL.
WHY DON'T YOU GUYS STOP GANGING UP ON HER AND TELL HER WHY WE'RE ALL HERE?
WHY US? YOU TELL HER.
WHY AM I ALWAYS THE ONE WHO HAS TO DO EVERYTHING?
TELL ME WHAT?
'CAUSE THIS WAS YOUR IDEA IN THE FIRST PLACE, VIOLET.
THAT'S RIGHT! BLAME ME! I KILLED AL CASTOR, I KILLED HERNAN SOLIS, I PUT MOM IN FUCKIN' JAIL...
HUH??
MOM'S IN JAIL, TONTA!
THAT'S THE WAY TO TELL HER, VI.
SO? I TOLD HER! JUST 'CAUSE YOU WERE TOO CHICKENSHIT TO DO IT, VIVIAN!
I'M CHICKENSHIT?? YOU CAN'T EVEN LOOK A GUY IN THE EYE WHEN YOU'RE GOING DOWN ON HIM AND LIFTING HIS WALLET AT THE SAME TIME!
BRINGING UP OLD SHIT, HUH? OK, THAT'S IT, YA FUCKING PIGSLUT...
VIVIAN VERSUS FATASS FUCKING WHORE, ROUND TWO!
XAIME 13
2.

DOGS FOLLOW DOGS

YOU GUYS FINISHED KILLING EACH OTHER?
YES, ISH. CAN WE GO NOW?
VIVIAN, WE CAN'T GO ANYWHERE UNTIL TONTA GETS BACK!

WHERE DID SHE GO?
DOWN THE ROAD. SHE WANTED TO BE ALONE.
LIKE THE LONER FUCK FACE SHE IS.

YOU TOLD HER?
EVERY-THING.

AND YOU LET HER GO OFF BY HERSELF?
FUCK...
FUCK YOU.

1.

YOU'RE NOT MY BROTHER, ISH MAN.
SORRY TO DISAPPOINT YOU.

I NEVER SEEN YOU AT CHRISTMAS AN' STUFF.
AH, I LEFT HOME BEFORE YOU WERE BORN. IT WAS TOO MUCH FOR ME AFTER MY DAD WAS GONE.

YOU WERE LITTLE. WHERE DID YOU GO?
LIVED WITH AN AUNT ON MY DAD'S SIDE.
GOT MY JOB AT THE COBIA CLUB WHEN I WAS 13. MR. SPROPP STEPPED IN LIKE SORT OF MY STEP-DAD.

VIVI THINKS MR. SPROPP HOOKED MOM UP WITH THE BURGLAR.
SHE'S ENTITLED TO BELIEVE THAT.

AM I ENTITLED TO BELIEVE MOM IS INNOCENT?
YEAH...

ISH!
MOM GOT BAIL AND WANTS THE KIDS HOME!
SHIT.
2.

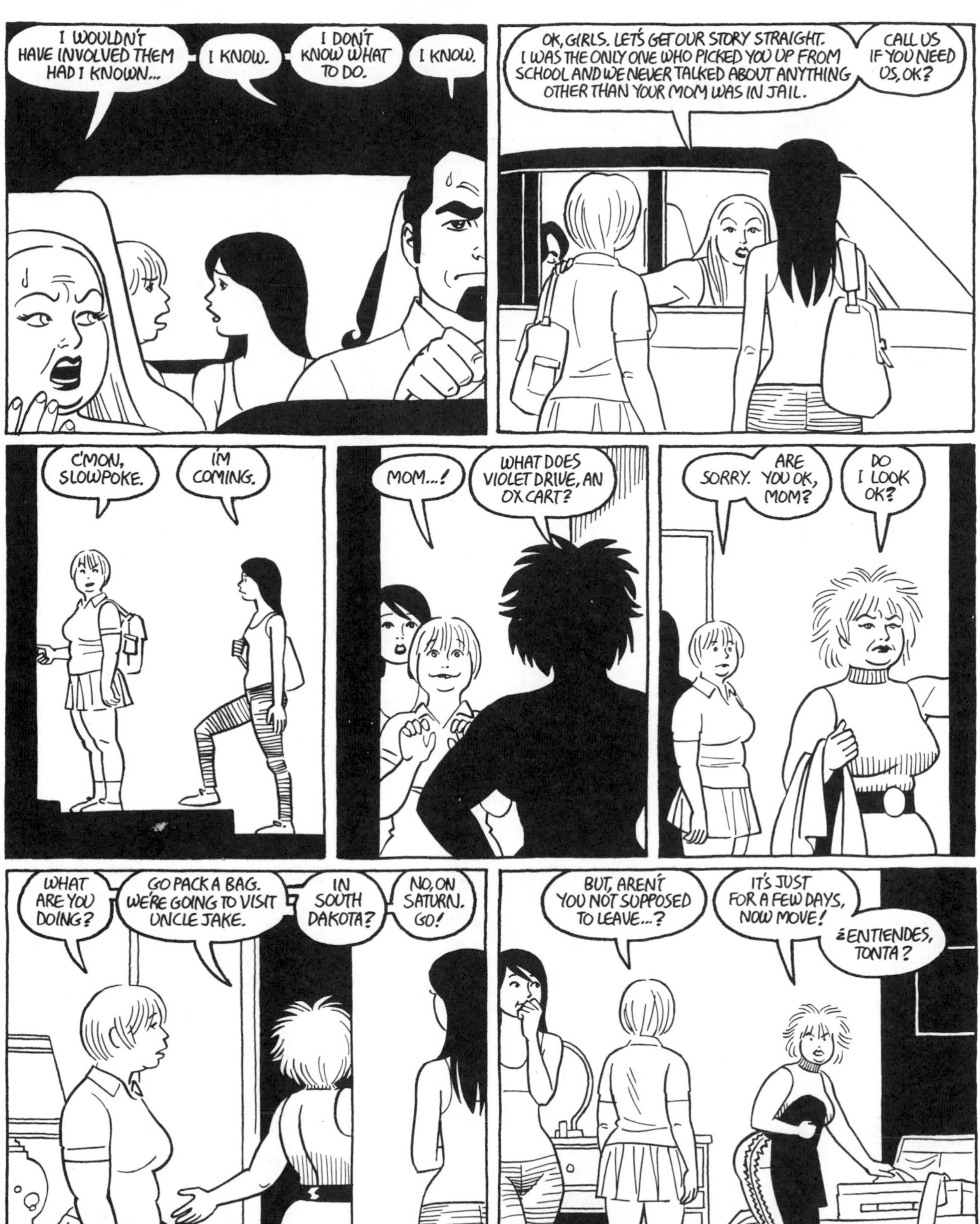
I WOULDN'T HAVE INVOLVED THEM HAD I KNOWN...
I KNOW.
I DON'T KNOW WHAT TO DO.
I KNOW.
OK, GIRLS. LET'S GET OUR STORY STRAIGHT. I WAS THE ONLY ONE WHO PICKED YOU UP FROM SCHOOL AND WE NEVER TALKED ABOUT ANYTHING OTHER THAN YOUR MOM WAS IN JAIL.
CALL US IF YOU NEED US, OK?
C'MON, SLOWPOKE.
I'M COMING.
MOM...!
WHAT DOES VIOLET DRIVE, AN OX CART?
SORRY.
ARE YOU OK, MOM?
DO I LOOK OK?
WHAT ARE YOU DOING?
GO PACK A BAG. WE'RE GOING TO VISIT UNCLE JAKE.
IN SOUTH DAKOTA?
NO, ON SATURN. GO!
BUT, AREN'T YOU NOT SUPPOSED TO LEAVE...?
IT'S JUST FOR A FEW DAYS, NOW MOVE!
¿ENTIENDES, TONTA?
3.

C'MON, MUÑECA. WE GOTTA...
WHAT ARE YOU DOING?
CALLING VIOLET.

OH NO, YOU DON'T. YOU'RE STAYING HERE, MU--
MUÑECA!

WHY AREN'T YOU PACKING?
WHERE'S MUÑECA?
SHE... UH...

¡CANALLA!
WELL, C'MON. WE'LL HAVE TO LEAVE WITHOUT HER.

¡TONTA!

XAIME 13 4.

WILLOW, WEEP NO MORE 2
BETO-2013

NICE ARM, BUT WHY SO ADAMANT ABOUT GETTING RID OF YOUR GRANDMOTHER'S HAMMER?
NOW MAYBE GRANDMA WON'T BE REMINDED OF ALL THE MISTAKES SHE'S MADE IN HER LIFE, DAD.
The HIVES

KILLER... I JUST WANT TO SAY I'M SORRY ABOUT...
I WAS JUST...
FORGET IT, DAD.
EVERYTHING'S ALL NORMAL AGAIN.
The HIVE

I'M LEAVING THE HAMMER HERE BECAUSE THIS IS WHERE MOM'S SISTER'S ASHES WERE SCATTERED.
YOU REMEMBER THAT I WAS NAMED AFTER MY TIA DORALIS?
SHE WAS A WRITER...
The HIVES
1

< REMIND YOUR DAUGHTER THAT SHE WON'T BE DRESSING LIKE THAT IN MY TOWN WHEN SHE'S 18, SENOR RIVERA. >
IGNORE HER, DAD.
< I GOT RID OF GRANDMA'S HAMMER AS A SYMBOL FOR ME QUITTING ACTING, GRAMPA. >
< AND IT'LL BE THERE IF YOU CHANGE YOUR MIND. >

< AND I'LL BE THERE FOR HER IN WHATEVER SHE DECIDES TO DO. >
< GOD HELP YOU IF LUBA FINDS OUT OTHERWISE, AMIGO. >

< YOU'RE VERY INTERESTED IN THE HOUSE ON THE HILL.
< BEFORE PIPO MOVED IN, IT BELONGED TO YOUR TIA DORALIS. >
< YEAH, I HEAR IT'S HAUNTED.
< WHAT ISN'T THESE DAYS? >

< FRITZ AND I HAVE NEVER HAD ANY GHOST EXPERIENCE IN THAT HOUSE, KILLER. >
< IT'S BECAUSE NEITHER OF YOU HAVE THE GHOST SENSITIVITY GENE LIKE I DO, PIPO. >

< AND SPEAKING OF FRITZ? >
I JUST FOUND OUT THAT HER DAD'S NAME IS HECTOR, DAD.
FUNNY WORLD, HUH?
2

ROSALBA, HECTOR.
FRITZ, MARIA.
NANCY
NANCY, DID YOU FART?
NO, AUNT FRITZI.
IT WAS A SIGN FROM GOD!
THE PHANTOM
GOD'S FART MAKES IT TO THE LOST JUNGLE.
AW, MAN.
GOD'S FART STINKS.

< WHY DO YOU WANT TO CALL THE BABY FRITZ, EVEN WHEN IT MIGHT BE A GIRL? >
< IT WORKS FOR A BOY OR GIRL, MARIA. >
< LITTLE FRITZI. >

< SINCE YOU LOOK SO MUCH LIKE 'AUNT FRITZI' FROM THE FUNNY PAPERS, CHANCES ARE THAT OUR BABY WILL TOO. >
< ROSALBA IS MY MOTHER'S NAME AND IF I'M HAVING A GIRL, SHE'LL BE ROSALBA TOO, HECTOR. >
NANCY

< WELL, IF WE'RE KEEPING IT IN YOUR FAMILY; BOY OR GIRL, LET'S NAME IT LUBA, LIKE FROM YOUR MYSTERIOUS PAST. >
< A BABY'S NOT AN IT, HECTOR! >
< AND THAT'S WHAT THE NAME LUBA SOUNDS LIKE! >
< AN IT! >

< ALL RIGHT THEN; ROSALBA IF SHE'S A GIRL. >
< BUT I'M STILL CALLING HER FRITZ. >
FRITZ...
3

I'M GOING TO STAR IN A REMAKE OF YOUR FULL-LENGTH MOVIE, MOM.
IT'LL GIVE US THE CHANCE TO OWN THE RIGHTS TO THE STORY.
THAT MOVIE I MADE WAS TRASH; WHY MAKE IT AGAIN?
IT'S MAKING SO MUCH MORE MONEY NOW THAN IT EVER HAS, MOM.
THE MOVIE YOU MADE BACK IN 1957 IS NOW A MIDNIGHT CULT FEATURE! PEOPLE LOVE YOU IN IT!
CAN'T IMAGINE WHY.
THEY WANT YOU TO APPEAR IN PERSON AT SCREENINGS, MOM. FAN REPORTERS ARE ALWAYS ASKING ME FOR EXCLUSIVE INTERVIEWS WITH YOU!
WELL, THEY CAN FORGET THAT, ALL RIGHT? AND DON'T TELL THEM WHERE TO FIND ME, EITHER.
4

SO, I NEED THE MONEY YOU THINK?
NO, OF COURSE NOT, IT'S JUST··
OH, FORGET IT.
I HAVE TO GO.
DON'T EXPECT ME TO SEE YOURS WHEN IT'S DONE.
ONCE IS ENOUGH FOR ME.
WHY DO I BOTHER?
DID YOU TELL HER THAT THEY WANT HER FOR A NEW MOVIE?
NO.
SHE WOULDN'T HAVE BEEN INTERESTED.
BYE.
LOOK, MAMA! I'M A STAR! I'M A STAR!
HA HAA HAAA!

< MOTHER MARIA AND DAUGHTER ROSALBA. >
< REALLY; FOR A SECOND I THOUGHT THIS WAS YOU DOING BOTH PARTS IN THE MOVIE. >
< OH, THAT FOOTAGE? >
< NO, THAT'S THE REAL ME AND MY MAMA BACK IN THE DAY, ONTHE AGAIN LOSING YET ANOTHER MOTHER/DAUGHTER TWIMTHUIT CONTETHT. >
< DIDN'T YOUR MOTHER EVER AGE, FRITZ? >
< LOOK WHO'TH TALKING. >
FRITZ
MARI
M.
< WHAT WATH THAT NOITHE, PIPO? >
< JUST GETTING UP OFF THE CHAIR, SCAREDY-CAT. >
< NO GHOSTS THAT TIME. >
WILLOW, WEEP NO MORE 3
BETO 2013
< ARE YOU ALONE? >
< THE SERVANTS HAVE ALL GONE HOME, SO IT'S JUST ME AND; WELL, YOU NEVER KNOW. >
FRIT
MA
M.
< JUTHT MAKE SURE A GHOTHT DOETHN'T GET IN BED WITH YOU. >
< FRITZ, THERE'S NO GHOSTS IN THIS OLD HOUSE; NOT EVEN YOUR NIECE. >
< KILLER'TH PROBABLY THE ONLY ONE THAT COULD TELL UTH FOR SURE. >

10TH ANNIVERSARY
FRITZ
MARIA M.

<AFTER THAT I DON'T THINK I LOVE YOU, LA LUBA DE PALOMAR.
<I KNOW I LOVE YOU, WOMAN.>
<I LOVE YOU, DOM.>

<THEY'RE NOT KIDDING THAT YOUR SISTER WENT WAY OVER THE TOP WITH PLAYING YOUR MOTHER; BODY, MIND AND SOUL, BUT MOSTLY BODY.>
<THE MOVIE WAS AS STUPID AND PHONEY AS I KNEW IT WOULD BE; AND FRITZ DIDN'T EVEN HAVE A LISP WHEN SHE PLAYED HERSELF.
<AH; DOOR.>

<PERFECT TIMING.>
<OOOH, YOU LOOK LIKE YOU JUST FINISHED WATCHING THE MOVIE.
<YOU COULD USE A BREAK, MAMA.>

<I WOULD PUT THE MOVIE IN THE HORROR CATEGORY.>
<HORRIBLE CATEGORY; SCI-FI FOR ACCURACY.>
<WE ALL HELD OUR BREATH FOR 10 YEARS FOR THE DAY YOU SAW THE MOVIE, MAMA.>
FOOO.

<THAT'S ONE REGULAR AND ONE DE-CAF?>
<DON'T MIX THEM UP.>

<OK, I SAW THE MOVIE; CAN WE DROP ALL THAT FOR GOOD NOW?
<I'M HAPPY LIVING IN THE U.S. WITH DOMINGO, BABY.
<BEST DECISION I EVER MADE WAS TO MOVE HERE.>
<MINE TOO, MAMA.>
2

< ALL THIS STUFF IS TWICE AS MUCH IN THE U.S., MAMA.>
< ANOTHER REASON FOR ME NEVER TO GO THERE.>
< OH, SURE; I SAY THAT, BUT WATCH; I'LL HAVE TO GO THERE FOR SOME REASON OR ANOTHER, GUADALUPE.>
< IT'S FATE.
< CAN'T FIGHT IT.>
< THE PERFUME THAT WOMAN'S WEARING...?
< I REMEMBER IT FROM SOMEWHERE.>
< YEAH, I SMELLED IT TOO, MAMA.
< REAL PRICEY.>
< THERE'S MORE RICH TOURISTS AROUND NOW THAN EVER, MAMA.>
< DOES LOOK THAT WAY, DORALIS.>
< THE WORLD'S GETTING SMALLER EVERY DAY.>
3

CRIMEN
SEIS

YOUR SISTER AND BROTHER ARE GOING THROUGH WITH THE TRIAL?
WELL, YEAH...

EVEN WITHOUT THEIR EXPERT WITNESS?
THEY GOT THEIR EXPERT WITNESS. OUR LITTLE SISTER SAW BUNNY CHURRO DO IT.

BUT THEY DON'T HAVE BUNNY CHURRO AND THE TRIAL IS TOMORROW.
THEY WILL. THE COPS ARE STILL LOOKING FOR HIM.

IT'S NOT TOO LATE FOR YOUR BROTHER TO BACK OUT.
HE WON'T BACK OUT. HE AND VIOLET ARE SUPER HARDCORE INTO IT.

I DON'T CARE ABOUT VIOLET BRUNET. YOU AND I BOTH KNOW SHE HAS ALWAYS BEEN IN IT FOR HERSELF, EVER SINCE SHE WAS SEVENTEEN PULLING TRICKS ON MY GOLF PARTNERS...
NO, IT, IS ISH IM WORRIED ABOUT...

THAT BOY HAS ALWAYS BEEN LIKE A SON TO ME. I'D HATE TO SEE HIM RIDICULED OVER THIS.
HE KNOWS WHAT HE'S DOING. HE'S WANTED THIS A LONG TIME.

HE'S TRYING TO FRY HIS OWN MOTHER!
HIS MOTHER! YOUR MOTHER...
MAYBE SHE'S GUILTY. YOU DON'T KNOW...

1.

I'VE KNOWN YOUR MOTHER LONGER THAN ANY OF YOU AND THAT SWEET, SWEET WOMAN DID NOT DO WHAT YOU'RE ACCUSING HER OF.
IT MUST BE BREAKING HER POOR HEART THAT HER OWN CHILDREN WOULD SEND HER TO THE ELECTRIC CHAIR.
THEY DON'T DO THAT HERE, DO THEY?
I'M DISAPPOINTED IN ISH, I REALLY AM. HE COULD LOSE HIS JOB OVER SOMETHING AS STUPID AS THIS. IT COULD RUIN HIM.
AND YOU...
GIVE HER BACK HER CLOTHES.
HURRY AND GET DRESSED. YOU LOOK LIKE...
...YOUR SISTER.
DON'T CALL ME ANY MORE, MR. SPROPP.
WHEN THIS IS OVER, TELEMARKETERS WON'T BE CALLING YOU...
WHAT DOES THAT MEAN?
HEY, WHAT DID YOU MEAN BY THAT?
WHAT...?
SLAM!
XAIME 13
2.

WE DID IT!
WE BEAT THEM BY A WHOLE SECOND!
SO WHAT IF WE GAVE TONTA A WHOLE LENGTH OF A POOL LEAD!

YOU DID IT, TONTA! WE DIDN'T WIN CIFS BUT THIS LAST RELAY WILL GIVE BRADBURY SOMETHING TO HANG OVER ST. MARTIN'S HEAD FOR YEARS TO COME!
HUBUBBAH HUBUBBAH HUBUBBAH... THANK... YOU... HUBBUBBAH...

OK, DOES EVERYBODY KNOW WHERE TO GO?
BERRY BERRY NICE ON SEPULVEDA!
BURY

IS TONTA AND GOMEZ COMING WITH US OR WITH HILLY?
NEITHER. THEY WENT TO THE COURT-HOUSE.
IS THAT THING STILL GOING ON? WHY DON'T THEY CONVICT HER ALREADY?
BITCH.
1.

WOW! IT'S A MEDIA CIRCUS!
KEEP DRIVING, GOMEZ.
I THOUGHT YOU WANTED ME TO BRING YOU...
NOT ANY MORE I DON'T! GO!
LA COUNTY
THIS IS SO AWESOME. IT'S JUST HOW I PICTURE MY NOVEL.
YOU'RE WRITING A NOVEL?
SORTA. I CAN'T DECIDE IF IT WILL BE A GRAPHIC NOVEL OR A NOVEL NOVEL.
I'M CALLING IT "TARZANA AND THE JEWELS OF MOPAR."
SO, IT'S LIKE TARZAN BUT A WOMAN? A JUNGLE GODDESS LIKE SHEENA OR JANN OR LORNA OR...
YEAH, BUT IS THAT HOMAGE OR IS IT FLAT OUT THIEVERY?
MAYBE YOU CAN CALL IT "TARZANA AN' THE FOREST SPIRIT."
YEAH, I COULD, I GUESS.
AND AT THE END, TARZANA CAN GET CLOBBERED OVER THE HEAD AND REALIZE SHE WAS THE FOREST SPIRIT THE WHOLE TIME.
I'M NOT THE FOREST SPIRIT.
OH, C'MON, GRETCH! GOMEZ IS NO FRICKIN' IDIOT...
BUT DIDN'T YOU SAY MYSTERIOUS STUFF WOULD HAPPEN MINUTES AFTER YOU TURNED YOUR BACK?
NO, NO. SHE'S RIGHT. IT WAS ME. I DID IT ALL.
2.

WELL, NOT ALL OF IT. THOSE STONERS HELPED A LITTLE...
NO, IT WAS ALL ME.
HAPPY?

GRETCH, I WAS JUST SAYING...
I KNOW. NOW YOU TALK.
HUH?

IT'S YOUR TURN. I'M DONE.
TALK.
UH...

D-DO YOU WANT TO SHOW ME MORE THINGS THE FOREST SPIRIT LEFT?
YOU'RE NOT EVEN SUPPOSED TO BE HERE.
DON'T PICK ON GOMEZ! IT'S NOT HER FAULT, GRETCH!

I TELL YOU WHO YOU CAN OR CAN'T BRING UP HERE!
YOU DON'T OWN THESE FRICKIN' WOODS, GRET-CHEN!

HEEEEEEYAAAAAAHHHH!
HEY! I WAS KIDDING!

I GUESS NOW'S NOT A GOOD TIME TO APOLOGIZE.
NAW, LET'S GIVE HER A FEW CENTURIES TO COOL DOWN.
3.

SHIT, I GOTTA GO BACK.
I LEFT MY FRICKIN' PHONE BY THE WATER.
WELL, DON'T GO BACK FOR IT NOW WHILE TARZANA RAGES!

I NEED IT. VIOLET GOT IT FOR ME TO KEEP ME UP ON THE TRIAL.
BE CAREFUL, TONTA.

DID YOU SEE GRETCHEN?
NO, BUT VIOLET SENT ME A TEXT...

THEY GOT A VERDICT.

XAIME 13

4.

CRIMEN
FINAL

MS. BRUNET HAS NO COMMENTS AT THIS TIME. SHE JUST WANTS TO BE WITH HER FAMILY RIGHT NOW.
THANK YOU.

HOW DO YOU LIKE THAT? STRAIGHT DOWN THE LINE. EVERY SINGLE ACCOUNT, NOT GUILTY, NOT GUILTY, NOT GUILTY...

IT'S ALL MY FAULT. I FUCKED IT UP FOR EVERY-BODY.
MOM'S FREE AND SHE GETS TO GO BACK TO HER NORMAL LIFE AND EVERYBODY ELSE IS FUCKED AND IT'S ALL BECAUSE OF MY BIG FUCKING BRIGHT IDEAS.

HOW DID I KNOW THEY'D PULL OUT THAT SHIT ABOUT HOW I CHANGED MY MIND AT MOM'S ORIGINAL TRIAL?
I BLITHERED LIKE A FUCKING IDIOT AND ISH WASN'T ANY BETTER.

THE SECOND AFTER THEY READ THE VERDICT, HE WAS OUTTA THERE LIKE A SHOT AND HE HASN'T RETURNED MY CALLS...
AND VIVI NEVER SHOWED UP AT ALL. SHE'S HIDING OUT WHO THE FUCK KNOWS WHERE.

BUT WHO CAN BLAME THEM? WE WERE SO IN OVER OUR HEADS, IT WAS LAUGHABLE. THE GUILTY BITCH GETS TO WALK BECAUSE HER FIRSTBORN IS A BUFFOON...

1.

HOLD ON, SOMEONE'S TEXTING ME.
OH, IT'S TONTA.
SO, I HOPE YOU GET THIS MESSAGE, JOLENA, BUT I MOSTLY HOPE BUNNY CHURRO SHOOTS YOU IN THE FUCKING HEAD AND SLITS YOUR MOTHERFUCKING THROAT.
BYE.
HI.
HI.
I SAW MUÑECA LEAVE WITH HER DAD.
YES, SHE'S NOT GOING BACK.
SO, I GUESS IT'S JUST LITTLE ALBY..
HE REALLY DOESN'T HAVE A CHOICE.
DID MY DAD DIE THE SAME WAY AS THE OTHERS?
NO, NO. HE DIED OF LEUKEMIA, REMEMBER?
WHAT ABOUT YOUR DAD?
KILLED HIMSELF.
CHRISTMAS IS GONNA BE FRICKIN' WEIRD.
XAIME 13
2.

AND PALOMAR AGAIN
BETO 2013
< I JUST FEEL CHEATED THAT I NEVER GOT TO MEET MY GREAT GRANDMA.
< SEEING HER ALIVE ON FILM MADE ME FEEL EVEN WORSE. >
< BEFORE PHOTOS AND MOVIES, RICH PEOPLE COULD HAVE PAINTINGS DONE OF FAMILY MEMBERS TO SHOW FUTURE GENERATIONS WHAT THE DEARLY DEPARTED LOOKED LIKE. >
< I NEVER GOT TO MEET MY TIA DORALIS, I NEVER GOT TO MEET OFELIA, NEVER GOT TO MEET YOUR SON SERGIO... >
< I NEVER GOT TO MEET MY MOM'S HUSBAND... >
< DON'T FORGET THAT YOUR BROTHER'S FATHER WAS MY HUSBAND FIRST.
< I'LL JUST BE A MINUTE. >
< I NEVER GOT TO MEET SPEEDY... >
?
< OH, FRITZ; COME ON...
< ARE YOU DRUNK?
< FRITZ, STOP CRYING... >

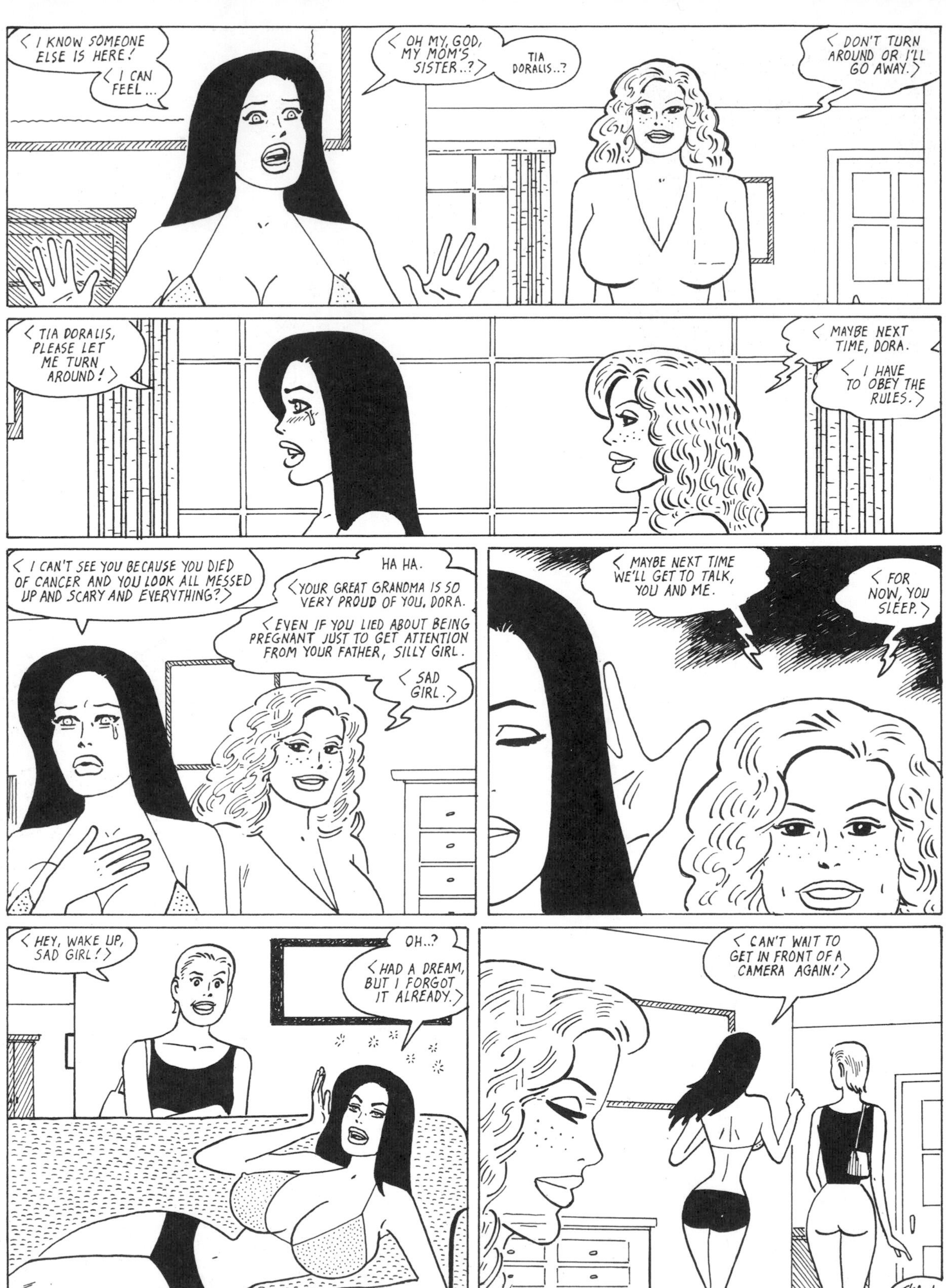
< I KNOW SOMEONE ELSE IS HERE!
< I CAN FEEL...
< OH MY, GOD, MY MOM'S SISTER..? >
TIA DORALIS..?
< DON'T TURN AROUND OR I'LL GO AWAY. >
< TIA DORALIS, PLEASE LET ME TURN AROUND! >
< MAYBE NEXT TIME, DORA.
< I HAVE TO OBEY THE RULES. >
< I CAN'T SEE YOU BECAUSE YOU DIED OF CANCER AND YOU LOOK ALL MESSED UP AND SCARY AND EVERYTHING? >
HA HA.
< YOUR GREAT GRANDMA IS SO VERY PROUD OF YOU, DORA.
< EVEN IF YOU LIED ABOUT BEING PREGNANT JUST TO GET ATTENTION FROM YOUR FATHER, SILLY GIRL.
< SAD GIRL. >
< MAYBE NEXT TIME WE'LL GET TO TALK, YOU AND ME.
< FOR NOW, YOU SLEEP. >
< HEY, WAKE UP, SAD GIRL! >
OH..?
< HAD A DREAM, BUT I FORGOT IT ALREADY. >
< CAN'T WAIT TO GET IN FRONT OF A CAMERA AGAIN! >
The End

RRRREGRESAMOS..

HOW'S LIFE IN TEMECULA, TONTA?
BESIDES LIVING WITH MY DEPRESSED, SUICIDAL, ALCOHOLIC, DRUG TAKING SISTER? IT SUCKS.
WHAT'S WITH THE SNOOKIS, MOSES? GIVE UP ON JUSTINS?

THEY GO TO YOUR SCHOOL. REMEMBER THAT DAY YOU MET YOUR NEW P.E. TEACHER?
DID I TELL YOU MY NEW SCHOOL SUCKS, TOO? I GUESS THAT COVERS THE REST.

I'VE NEVER SEEN THE BARN SO PACKED.
ITS ALL THESE NEW KIDS. EVER SINCE THE NEW E.P.
WHO KNEW OOOT COULD GET ANY MORE ROCK STAR.
1.

TONTA.
CHATA.

I GUESS SHE DOESN'T HATE YOU ANY MORE.
WHATEVSIES.

WHO'S NEXT? WHO'S NEXT? BLACK WIDOW B

MY KITCHEN IS CLEAN SO PROUD OF ITS SHEEN...

DON'T SPOIL MY DAY OFF BY STAINING IT WITH ME...

WHO'S NEXT? YOU'RE NEXT! WHOSE VEX? HER HEX!

2.

BLACK WIDOW... BLACK WIDOW...
BLACK WIDOW...?

BLACK WID
BLACK WI

BLACK WIDOW...

BLACK WIDOW GOT MY BACK MARKED WITH AN X!

C'MON, TONTA!
BRING HER, VIVI!
I'M TRYING TO, VIOLET!

YOU WANNA GO IN THE WATER, TONTA?
IT'S OK, I'LL HOLD YOUR HAND.
SHE'S A SCAREDY CAT, JUST LIKE HER HALF-BROTHER.

3.

OW!
WHAT NOW, MOSQUITOS?

NO, SOME ASSBITE IS THROWING THINGS!
HEY!

WHO'S A SCAREDY CAT, NOW?
ISH, YOU FISH!
YOU ALMOST HIT TONTA!

HOW DID YOU FIND US?
I FOLLOWED YOU GUYS FOR A LONG TIME.
LAST ONE IN THE WATER IS A FISH HEAD!

WHAT WAS THAT SHRILL SOUND AS IF I DIDN'T KNOW?
MAMA!
AW, I JUST GOT HERE.

COME WITH US, ISH. WE'RE GETTING BIG STICKS.
NO FUCKING WAY.
WHO'S A SCAREDY CAT NOW?

C'MON, TONTA! BIG STICKS!
SO LONG, FISH HEAD.
XAIME 13 4.